THE PROMISED LAND

TRICENTENNIAL STUDIES, NUMBER 1

This volume is part of a series of *Tricentennial Studies*, published by the University of South Carolina Press on behalf of the South Carolina Tricentennial Commission, to commemorate the founding of South Carolina in 1670.

THE
PROMISED
LAND

The History of the South Carolina
Land Commission
1869-1890

Carol K. Rothrock Bleser

Published for the South Carolina Tricentennial Commission
by the University of South Carolina Press, Columbia, S. C.

In Memory of
STEPHEN F. FOGLE

ACKNOWLEDGMENTS

IT IS A PLEASURE TO ACKNOWLEDGE the kind assistance of many friends and colleagues who made this book possible. I particularly wish to thank Professor Eric L. McKitrick of Columbia University, to whose inspiring guidance and keen criticism whatever merit this book possesses is largely due. I am grateful, too, to Professors James Shenton, Sigmund Diamond, Walter Metzger, and Richard Bone, all of Columbia University, for reading the manuscript in its dissertation form and for offering valuable suggestions. Professor Eugene Genovese, of Sir George Williams University, read the revised manuscript and raised some questions that I am sure in the answering made it a better study. Professors George Rogers, of the University of South Carolina, and Robert Ackerman, of Erskine College, also read and commented on the completed work. Others have rendered important assistance by reading portions of it.

I am most deeply indebted to Mr. Charles Lee, the director of the South Carolina Department of Archives and History, who suggested the topic. The aid and interest of Mr. Lee and his staff facilitated the gathering of the research material, and, furthermore, made my stay at the Archives a very pleasurable experience. I am most appreciative, too, for the assistance of Mr. William McDowell, deputy director, and of the reference archivist, Miss Wylma Wates. I also wish to thank the library staffs of the South Caroliniana Library, University of South Carolina, South Carolina Historical Society, Charleston Library Society, Duke University, University of North Carolina at Chapel Hill, Columbia University, Adelphi Suffolk College, New York Public Library, Library of Congress, and the National Archives. The late Mr. Calhoun Mays, Sr., and his daughter-in-law Mrs. Marshall Mays rendered much assistance. They shared with me their knowledge of Promised Land (a former Land Commission tract) and guided me through this community, making possible interesting interviews with descendants of the original settlers.

I am indebted, moreover, to the Woodrow Wilson Foundation for awarding me a dissertation fellowship for the year 1963–1964. This generous grant provided me with the free time necessary to complete the research and write a first draft of the manuscript. A postdoctoral fellowship from the National Endowment for the Humanities awarded for the academic year 1967–1968 made it possible for me to revise the study and prepare it for publication.

Finally, to my husband Edward, who listened, critically analyzed, drew maps, and forbore, and to our son Gerald, who never lost hope that I would finish, go my love and appreciation.

C. K. R. B.

CONTENTS

INTRODUCTION

R ECONSTRUCTION IN SOUTH CAROLINA continues to exercise an undeniable fascination upon the minds of historians. In the past so much attention was focused on South Carolina that it became the classic example of Radical Reconstruction. Nevertheless in recent years students of the period, aware of the relevance of Reconstruction to the current racial situation and motivated in part by the approaching centennial, began reconsidering the era in the light of newer insights and previously unavailable evidence. A number of excellent studies on the history of the Palmetto State during Reconstruction have appeared as a result of this reappraisal, but little has been written about the South Carolina Land Commission.

Congressional Reconstruction began with the passage of the Military Reconstruction Acts in March, 1867, calling for elections in which adult Negro males could vote for or against a convention to reorganize the state government; whites disqualified under the proposed Fourteenth Amendment were excluded from voting. In South Carolina, Benjamin F. Perry, provisional governor after the war, urged white South Carolinians to block the calling of a convention by registering and voting against the convention—for it would not assemble unless a majority of those registered endorsed it. In one of a series of letters published in the newspapers, Perry warned that whites who voted for a convention "will be voting the ultimate confiscation of their lands and their political rights as surely as they are voting away their honor as men and Carolinians."[1] Other prominent men in the state, including Wade Hampton and James L. Orr, disagreed with Perry; they favored calling the convention to end military Reconstruction. During the spring of 1867 these men attempted to persuade Negroes to vote with the Democrats to elect conservative delegates to the convention.

By the middle of August a reaction had taken place. Hampton, Orr, and their associates, discouraged by the coolness of the Negro electorate, had come to agree with Perry that it was preferable to remain indefinitely under military rule than to accept the terms of the Republicans.[2]

At the election held on November 19 and 20, 1867, most conservative whites stayed away from the polls "under silent protest," hoping enough Negroes would also stay away to form a majority of those registered and thereby defeat the convention call. But 66,418 Negroes out of a total registration of 80,550 flocked to the polls and voted unanimously "For a convention." Of the 46,882 whites registered, only 4,628 voted—2,278 "Against a convention" and 2,350 for it.[3]

1. Charleston *Courier*, May 4, 1867.
2. Wade Hampton to A. L. Burt, n.d., Wade Hampton Papers, Duke University, Durham, N.C., cited in Joel Williamson, *After Slavery: The Negro in South Carolina During Reconstruction, 1861–1877* (Chapel Hill: The University of North Carolina Press, 1965), p. 407 n.; Wade Hampton to James Conner, August 1, 1867, James Conner Papers, South Carolina Historical Society, Charleston; Hampton Jarrell, *Wade Hampton and the Negro: The Road Not Taken* (Columbia: University of South Carolina Press, 1949), pp. 19–25, 216–18; Lillian A. Kibler, *Benjamin F. Perry: South Carolina Unionist* (Durham: Duke University Press, 1946), pp. 449–60; Eric L. McKitrick, *Andrew Johnson and Reconstruction* (Chicago: The University of Chicago Press, 1960), p. 246.
3. Henry W. Ravenel, Private Journal, 1859–1883, November 19–20, 1867, Manuscript Division, South Caroliniana Library, Columbia; Kibler, p. 461; Francis B. Simkins and Robert H. Woody, *South Carolina During Reconstruction* (Chapel Hill: The University of North Carolina, 1932), p. 89.

The constitutional convention assembled on January 14, 1868, in Charleston—where the Ordinance of Secession had been adopted and signed. Seventy-six of the 124 delegates were Negroes. Although the Negroes had acquired from the white man a passion for owning land, Perry's prediction that if a convention were held the property of the whites would be confiscated for the benefit of the freedmen was not borne out. After much debate about a land distribution program, the delegates worked out a program whereby the state would purchase land and sell it to Negroes on a long-term payment plan. They instructed the next legislature to create a state land commission designed to help the landless acquire homesteads. The convention put the dream of Negro landownership on paper.

On March 27, 1869, the South Carolina legislature accordingly established the Land Commission, thereby beginning a unique experiment. The importance of land to the former slaves cannot be exaggerated. They had emerged from bondage destitute, "without land, without shelter, without a legal claim even to the clothes on their backs."[4] Since land was the principal form of wealth in the South, owning property was the only effective means by which freedmen could achieve lasting economic equality. The Palmetto State was the only Southern state to promote the redistribution of land for the benefit of the freedmen.

Until recently very little was known about the Land Commission experiment. It was assumed that the records of the Land Commission had been destroyed until in 1961 a member of the staff at the South Carolina Archives opened some unmarked cartons and discovered the bulk of the missing records. Since that time other records and the minutes of the Land

4. Kenneth M. Stampp, *The Era of Reconstruction, 1865–1877* (New York: Alfred A. Knopf, 1965), p. 122.

Commission have been found in the basement of the Sinking Fund Commission building, in the General Services Department, and in other boxes stored at the Archives. The Land Commission ledgers, together with the sorted and unsorted Governors' Papers, the Loose Paper Files of 1866–1877, as well as unfiled loose papers, the Secretary of State's Land Commission letters, the Sinking Fund Commission's minutes and ledgers, and numerous manuscript sources, provide an abundance of primary source materials concerning the operations of the Land Commission.

In its first phase the state agency can be traced from its humanitarian inception, through its implementation by law, its organizational structure, and its transactions, to its frauds and their exposure by the Republicans themselves. The second, or reform stage began under the banner of Republicanism. The so-called "carpetbaggers," "scalawags," and "ignorant blacks" in the state legislature played a vital role in reclaiming the program by abolishing the office of land commissioner in February, 1872, and transferring the duties of the land commissioner to the secretary of state. The honest and assiduous Negro secretaries of state during the period 1872–1876, with the aid of the Land Commission Advisory Board, redeemed the land reform program from the once truthful imputation of being a "gigantic folly." Yet short-lived was the triumph. Although the experiment did not end with the overthrow of the Republican government in 1877, the Redeemers remolded the institution. In the third stage of the history of the Land Commission, the Redeemers, committed to a policy of retrenchment, efficiency, and economy, enacted new legislation subjecting all Land Commission sales to the direction of the Sinking Fund Commission. Henceforth sales were to help extinguish the state debt. Other distortions of the Land Commission Act were the increasing harshness of the conditions of sale and the stricter observance of collection schedules. During the 1880's fewer Negroes took up residence under the new terms of sale, while many already settled upon the tracts were evicted. Deprived of their small farms, many settlers were drawn into sharecropping.

By about 1890 South Carolina abandoned the experiment; nevertheless, something positive remained. Though many of the Land Commission settlers were deprived of their land, some individuals retained their holdings. In fact, some Land Commission tracts are still held together by independent farmers who are descendants of the original owners. One such tract, the "Promised Land," is described in the Epilogue. After 1890, within the boundaries of these communities, the Negroes may have been free to develop economically and socially in virtual independence of the whites, and in time they came to be described as a "black yeomanry."

The Land Commission is an ideal case for the study of a Reconstruction institution. In addition, since the Commission is entwined with the history of South Carolina during Reconstruction and Redemption, it also provides a vehicle for reevaluating aspects of this entire period.

Moreover, it is hoped that this study will illuminate one segment of American Negro history and contribute to a better understanding of the continuing race problem. Over fifty years ago, W. E. B. Du Bois remarked that "to give the Negro only the ballot without the land as an economic underpinning was to end a civil war by beginning a race feud."[5]

The South Carolina Land Commission, had it been success-

5. W. E. B. Du Bois, *The Souls of Black Folk: Essays and Sketches* (Chicago, 1918), p. 38, cited in Martin Abbott, *The Freedmen's Bureau in South Carolina, 1865–1872* (Chapel Hill: The University of North Carolina Press, 1967), p. 65. Although Abbott's book is seldom cited in the footnotes, it is of extreme importance. Throughout this study his work is cited in its unpublished doctoral dissertation form.

ful, might have enabled the black landowner to retain political and civil rights even during the post-Reconstruction era
and could have had great impact on his standard of living, his
status, and his long-range contributions to the community.
And perhaps the experiment would not have ended there in
South Carolina.

THE PROMISED LAND

CHAPTER I

The Sea Island Experiment
and Beyond

O F ALL THE SOUTHERN STATES during Reconstruction, South
    Carolina was unique in establishing a state agency, the
Land Commission, to give freedmen an opportunity to become landowners. The origin of the state's commitment toward making former slaves freeholders of their native soil is
to be found in the military occupation of the Sea Islands by
Union forces during the Civil War.

As early as November 7, 1861, Port Royal and St. Helena's
Parish were occupied by Federal troops, forcing the prosperous Sea Island planters to abandon their plantations and flee
into the interior. The approximately 10,000 slaves left behind[1]
were declared "contrabands of war." The term "contraband"
(property subject to seizure) provided a kind of interim basis
upon which the North could extend protection to Negro refugees without unduly alienating the Border States.[2]

1. U. S. War Department, *Official Records of the War of Rebellion* (Washington: Government Printing Office, 1892), Series I, VI, pp. 4–6, hereafter cited
as *War of Rebellion*.
2. George R. Bentley, *A History of the Freedmen's Bureau* (Philadelphia:

The Federal forces sought to fill the vacuum created by the hurried departure of the Confederates. On Hilton Head "contraband" labor was used to build extensive earthwork defenses against the expected counterattack, which never came. The mounds of earth still testify to the military's first profitable utilization of Negro labor.[3] Daily their numbers increased as slaves who had slipped through the Confederate lines arrived to seek sanctuary with the Union troops garrisoned on the islands. The presence of so many idle and disorganized Negroes created an acute problem for the army. Who was to assume responsibility for the contrabands? How could they be fed, housed, and clothed in the absence of their masters without government aid? These and a dozen other perplexing questions confronted the War Department. Something had to be done immediately.

The War Department rid itself of the problem by shifting the burden of responsibility to the Treasury Department. Secretary of the Treasury, Salmon P. Chase, acted at once, appointing agents to collect the abandoned cotton crops and to prepare for new crops to be planted.[4] At the same time, Secretary Chase sent his close personal friend Edward L. Pierce, a young Boston attorney, to investigate the condition of the Negroes. Pierce spent two weeks at Port Royal and submitted a formal report of his findings to Chase. Pierce stated that the blacks were capable of cultivating the cotton crops and were

University of Pennsylvania, 1955), p. 2; Willie Rose, *Rehearsal for Reconstruction: The Port Royal Experiment* (New York: Bobbs-Merrill Co., 1964), p. 15. *Rehearsal for Reconstruction* is a definitive study of the Civil War experiment undertaken at Port Royal to prepare the Sea Island Negroes for the transition from slave to citizen. Mrs. Rose's thesis is that the "rehearsal" shaped the Federal government's policy for Reconstruction undertaken after the war.

3. "Fort Sherman," Historical Marker erected by the Hilton Head Island Historical Society, 1961.

4. Guion Griffis Johnson, *A Social History of the Sea Islands: With Special Reference to St. Helena Island, South Carolina* (Chapel Hill: The University of North Carolina Press, 1930), p. 160.

willing to work for the government; however, the Sea Island Negroes required the supervision, aid, and protection of capable white men. He proposed that superintendents be carefully chosen to manage the plantations and also to prepare the Negroes for citizenship.[5] Unofficially, he suggested to Chase that with the superintendents should go ministers and teachers to instruct the Negroes, to elevate them religiously, morally, and socially, as well as to train them in the ways of free labor.

Pierce's "social experiment" did not receive official approval in Washington, but private citizens in Boston and New York launched a drive to undertake the mission. Committees were organized to interview and to select superintendents, teachers, and ministers, and funds were raised to support them.

On March 3, 1862, fifty-three men and women sailed from New York, and within two weeks of their arrival in the Sea Islands, each teacher, minister, and superintendent had been assigned a task and was at work.[6] Generally a superintendent had five or six plantations and as many as five hundred Negroes to supervise. The new system of labor differed in two important aspects from the ante-bellum regime: under no circumstance was the whip to be used to discipline the workers, and the Negroes were to be paid for their labor.[7] While the superintendents were busy with the crops, the teachers had to overcome the Negroes' initial reluctance to become their pupils. Soon it became apparent to all that more recruits were needed if the experiment was to succeed.

Citizens of Philadelphia undertook to strike a blow for the cause of freedom. Two days after Pierce's band sailed, the Port Royal Relief Committee was formed in that city. By April, the

5. *Ibid.*, pp. 160–64; Rose, pp. 21–29.
6. Rose, pp. 21–77.
7. Johnson, pp. 161–69.

Philadelphia recruits and supplies were on their way southward. Laura M. Towne, representing the Philadelphia committee, set up a school at Frogmore on St. Helena Island to train Negroes for freedom. She was soon joined by her friend Ellen Murray. Harriet Ware began her work among the Negroes at the same time.[8] Others joined them. By 1863, twelve schools had been established and were attended by 2,500 black people.[9]

The societies paid all salaries for the first four months of the experiment. After that, the Treasury Department paid the superintendents, but the salaries and expenses of the teachers and ministers remained the responsibility of the benevolent societies of the North. As the occupation continued, the goals of the missionary-teachers expanded. For instance, instructing their charges in the ways of economic freedom was placed on a par with providing education and religious training. Moreover, they considered the possession of land essential if the slaves were to be made responsible citizens in the post-bellum economic structure, but their limited resources were not adequate for so broad an enterprise.

It was the arrival at Beaufort of United States tax commissioners that inadvertently provided the means by which a permanent black yeoman class was created on the Sea Islands. On August 8, 1861, Congress levied a direct tax on each state to provide revenue to carry on the war. South Carolina's tax assessment was $363,570.66.[10] The following year Congress passed acts of forfeiture for the non-payment of the Federal

8. Rupert Sergeant Holland (ed.), *Letters and Diary of Laura M. Towne: Written from the Sea Islands of South Carolina 1862–1884* (Cambridge: Riverside Press, 1912); Elizabeth Ware Pearson (ed.), *Letters from Port Royal: Written at the time of the Civil War* (Boston: W. B. Clarke Co., 1906). The letters and diaries of Laura Towne and Harriet Ware form an indispensable source of primary material of the Sea Island experiment.

9. Johnson, p. 180.

10. U. S. *Statutes at Large*, XII, pp. 294–95.

tax of 1861. Three commissioners arrived at Beaufort to assess taxes. They placed advertisements warning rebel owners to appear, take the oath of allegiance, and pay the tax or forfeit their property. Only two complied.[11] Consequently, the lands of St. Helena and thousands of acres on Port Royal came into the possession of the Federal government to be sold for taxes. The commissioners scheduled a series of public sales to begin in February, 1863.

The missionaries were distressed. They opposed turning over the estates to private speculators just as the social experiment was beginning to show some success. They insisted that if the estates were to be sold, some land should be reserved for the Negroes. Laura Towne appealed to General Rufus Saxton, the military governor of the Sea Islands. Could not Saxton request General Hunter, commanding general of the Department of the South, to postpone the sales until the government's views on pre-emption might be ascertained? "General Saxton caught at the idea,"[12] and Hunter agreed to issue an order postponing the sale. The tax commissioners, however, took the matter to the War Department, and the order came back to proceed with the sales.[13]

When on March 9, 1863, 76,775 acres were put up for sale, the teachers and superintendents were relieved that no unsavory land sharks appeared. The government bid in for 60,296 acres, and "loyal citizens" purchased the remainder. Several plantations, totaling around 2,000 acres, were purchased cooperatively by the Negroes for slightly less than one dollar an acre.[14]

Edward S. Philbrick of Brookline, Massachusetts, was the

11. Elizabeth H. Andrews (ed.), "Charles Howard Family Domestic History," typed copy deposited at South Carolina Archives, Columbia, p. 108.
12. Holland (ed.), pp. 100–01.
13. *Ibid.*, p. 103.
14. Rose, pp. 214–15.

chief private purchaser. He had come out with Pierce's band as a superintendent. When it became apparent that the land sales would take place, he had persuaded a group of Bostonians to join him in the enterprise of carrying on the free labor experiment under private auspices. Philbrick purchased eleven plantations, totaling 8,000 acres, on St. Helena Island and employed freedmen to cultivate his cotton crops. To the satisfaction of the Boston joint stock company, Philbrick, from an investment of approximately $50,000, netted $81,000 in a single year.[15] Although motivated primarily toward making the venture a financial success, Philbrick did demonstrate that the Negro could successfully be integrated into the free labor force.[16]

Even though the bulk of the land bid in for the United States was reserved for military, naval, educational, and charitable purposes, the missionary-teachers hoped that any surplus land would be put in the hands of the Negroes. The government did in fact attempt to carry out such a policy. Late in December, President Lincoln and Secretary Chase gave authority for the survey of 60,000 acres of land—with the exception of certain lands set aside for military or educational purposes—into twenty and forty acre tracts, to be sold to the heads of Negro families for not less than $1.25 an acre. Two-fifths of the price was due on pre-emption, and the remainder upon receipt of the deed.[17]

The opportunity to buy land of their own created much excitement among the Negroes. During the month of January, 1864, the tax commissioners were inundated with pre-emption

15. *Ibid.*, Appendix, p. 434.

16. William H. Pease and Jane H. Pease, *Black Utopia: Negro Communal Experiments in America* (Madison, Wisconsin: The State Historical Society of Wisconsin, 1963), pp. 139–41.

17. Holland (ed.), p. 129; Pearson (ed.), pp. 243–44; Rose, p. 285; Williamson, p. 57.

claims from all over the Sea Islands.[18] But the pre-emption plan failed. Although the missionary-teachers continued to urge the Negroes to stake out claims to the land, the tax commissioners and speculators now beseiged their friends in the government to reverse the order of December. Early in February, 1864, a new order from Washington brought disappointing news to the freedmen: "Pre-emptions don't count, sell by auction."[19] This the tax commissioners hastily proceeded to do, with the result that in 1864 most purchases were made by speculators. Only a small amount of land was reserved for Negro purchasers under the category of "charitable purposes." The number of Negro buyers and the acreage involved are not known, but by June, 1865, 347 purchases had been made by the Negroes on St. Helena Island. The majority (243) "bought ten acres: 166 paying $1.50 an acre and 72 paying $1.25, the other five paying from $2.00 to $6.50 an acre. The highest price paid for any tract was $350 for twenty acres. In only two instances did purchasers buy land as low as $1.00 an acre."[20] Probably of the 2,300 purchasers of tax lands on Port Royal and St. Helena Islands no more than 500 were Negroes.[21]

Although hope had dwindled, it was revived during the last year of the war by General William T. Sherman's Field Order No. 15. Issued in January, 1865, Sherman's order was one of expediency, yet it did much to revive the freedmen's belief that they were to be beneficiaries of a Federal land program. Sherman's order set aside for the Negroes who had followed his army all the Sea Islands from Charleston to Port Royal,

18. Large Box marked "Pre-emption Claims," Records U. S. Direct Tax Commission, S. C., cited in Rose, pp. 286–87.

19. Pearson (ed.), p. 254; Rose, p. 290; Williamson, p. 58.

20. MSS, *Heads of Families Certificate Books*, U. S. Treasury Department Archives, cited in Johnson, p. 187; Holland (ed.), pp. xv–xvi.

21. George Tindall, *South Carolina Negroes, 1877–1900* (Columbia: University of South Carolina Press, 1952), p. 100; Williamson, p. 58.

and adjoining lands to a distance of 30 miles inland.[22] General Rufus Saxton executed the order and divided 485,000 acres among 40,000 Negroes. They were given, however, only "possessory" titles. As soon as the war ended, the returning ex-Confederates challenged the validity of the titles, and applied to the Freedmen's Bureau for the return of these lands.

When it became clear that President Andrew Johnson expected to be extremely generous in reconstructing the Southern states, conceiving "the pardoning power and the reconstructing power as one and the same,"[23] and that his basic test was simply repentance, Sherman himself repented. In a letter to the President, Sherman placed the responsibility for the issuance of his field order on his superior, the Secretary of War, Edwin Stanton. According to the general, the Secretary had come to Savannah and conferred with him as to the best method of providing for the Negroes who had followed the army from the interior of Georgia, for those who had already congregated on Hilton Head Island, and for those who were still coming into his lines. After their discussions Stanton had interviewed a number of Negroes and was convinced that the freedmen could, by means of the abandoned plantations on the Sea Islands, became self-sufficient. At Stanton's request, Sherman had drawn up a plan for redistributing the land among the Negroes. After Stanton had made many revisions, the final document had been issued as Sherman's Field Order No. 15. Sherman later disclaimed any intention of devising an ultimate solution to the problem of Negro landownership. He insisted to the President, "I merely aimed to make provisions for the negroes who were absolutely dependent on us, leaving the validity of their possession to be determined by after

22. *War of Rebellion*, Series I, XLVII, Part II, pp. 60–62.
23. Eric L. McKitrick, *Andrew Johnson and Reconstruction* (Chicago: The University of Chicago Press, 1960), p. 149.

events or legislation."[24] In the final analysis, the expedient land policy initiated by Stanton and formulated by Sherman brought only confusion and disappointment.

Neither Andrew Johnson nor Congress ever seriously contemplated validating the possessory titles to the forty acre tracts. In fact, Johnson had issued orders that all lands not sold directly by the Direct Tax Commission were to be returned to their former owners, if the owners took the oath of allegiance, obtained presidential pardon, and paid the tax.[25] And, even though Thaddeus Stevens advocated to his colleagues in the House of Representatives that they pass legislation confiscating the land of Confederates owning more than 2,000 acres, Congress had not the slightest intention of passing so revolutionary a measure as a confiscation bill.[26]

There were, however, deliberate delays in the restoration of property in South Carolina. General O. O. Howard, chief of the Freedmen's Bureau, continued to distribute as much land as possible to the freedmen, hoping thereby to commit the government to his policy by presenting it with a *fait accompli*.[27] Since Howard refused all applications for the restoration of property in the districts covered by Sherman's field order, South Carolinians sent petitions to the President urging him to help them recover their plantations. According to the petitioners of Edisto, John's, and Wadmalaw Islands, they had complied with the presidential orders governing the restoration of confiscated property, but the military authorities at Charleston continued to refuse their applications. The planters at first smarted under military postponements and then

24. Sherman to Johnson, February 2, 1866, cited in the Columbia *Daily Phoenix*, February 9, 1866.

25. Bentley, pp. 92–93, 95.

26. E. Merton Coulter, *The South During Reconstruction, 1865–1877* (Baton Rouge: Louisiana State University Press, 1947), pp. 66–68.

27. Bentley, pp. 92–93, 95; Williamson, pp. 80–81.

began to fear that the delay would become permanent and that their lands would never be returned to them. They wrote to the President:

> It is proper that we should bring to the notice of your Excellency . . . a rumor which is becoming prevalent, and which has lately reached us; to the effect, that the authorities having charge of this business are *running off our lands* on the Islands, herein alluded to, into seven acre and forty acre lots, and *dividing them among the negroes*, who are congregating in that neighborhood . . . . Even the *rumor* of such a scheme is scheduled to excite the most painful anxiety among your petitioners; as the subsistence of their families for the future is involved in it.[28]

In addition, the petitioners blamed the government's vacillating land policy for the dislocation of the state's labor system. The freedmen, in pursuit of cheap and easily obtainable lands, were "abandoning in large numbers, their contracts for the present crop, whilst rushing to the Sea Islands to obtain lands . . . ."[29] Brigadier General Ralph Ely, a sub-agent of the Freedmen's Bureau at Columbia, South Carolina, supported the planters' testimony. Ely wrote to his chief, General Howard, urging him to abandon his program of dispensing land. Only by restoring the coastal plantations to the original owners, he declared, could the migration of freedmen to the coast be stopped. Thus the Negroes, no longer lured on by free lands, would be forced to remain where they were and to sign labor contracts with the planters.[30]

Before Howard had time to reply to Ely, President Johnson acted in behalf of the petitioners. He commanded Howard to

28. Petition of the Planters on Sea Islands to Andrew Johnson, September 23, 1865, Edward M. Stoeber Papers, Manuscript Division, South Caroliniana Library, Columbia, cited hereafter as S.C.L.

29. *Ibid.*

30. Ely to Howard, September 22, 1865, Edward M. Stoeber Papers.

obey his order and restore all land that had not been *sold outright* by the Direct Tax Commission if the owners had complied with his directives.[31] Johnson's order, however, did allow loyal freedmen to remain upon the tracts until their crops had been harvested.[32] The Negroes, however, misunderstood Johnson's directive. They assumed that by permitting them to remain through the winter of 1865–1866, Johnson was really committing himself to Negro landownership. While waiting for the President's plan to unfold, the Negro settlers refused to make contracts with the impatient planters.

Freedmen throughout the South steadfastly believed that the United States government planned to give each former slave "forty acres and a mule." Although the rumor was widespread, only in South Carolina on the Sea Islands had Negroes become landowners. Consequently, it was in South Carolina that the postwar expectation of Federal distribution of land was greatest. Moreover, Howard's failure to carry out immediately Johnson's restoration plan reinforced the Negroes' misconceptions. To combat the rumor, Howard—who was himself partly responsible for the confusion—issued and reissued orders, bulletins, and circulars to officers and agents of the Freedmen's Bureau. He instructed his men to correct the erroneous impression of "forty acres and a mule," and to urge the Negroes to make contracts for labor in 1866. Special effort was made to convince the freedmen crowding the South Carolina coast that they could acquire land only through purchase.[33] Agents and officers of the Freedmen's Bureau talked, cajoled,

31. Bentley, pp. 92–95; Rose, p. 351.
32. Printed circular issued by the Assistant Commissioner of the Freedmen's Bureau for South Carolina and Georgia, September 28, 1865, Freedmen File, South Carolina Archives, Columbia, cited hereafter as S.C.A.
33. Printed circulars 5, 21, 75, Bureau of Refugees, Freedmen and Abandoned Lands, South Carolina and Georgia, October 19, November 11, December 15, 1865, Miscellaneous Papers, 1865–1866, S.C.A.

and threatened, all to no avail. The South Carolina Negroes chose to listen to other counsel.

Into the small communities, meanwhile, had come strangers to swindle the ignorant blacks. They sought out those who possessed some cash, and to them showed packages of red, white, and blue sticks, four to a package. "Get up before light," the strangers said, "plant a stick at the four corners of any piece of land not over a mile square and the land is yours." The sharpsters warned, "be wary or the rebels will get ahead of you."[34] Packages at five dollars each were sold quickly.

New Year's, 1866, brought only disappointment. Since the Negroes refused to give up the land peaceably, squads of soldiers went through the Sea Island plantations in February forcing the Negroes who were without valid claims either to contract with the planters or to leave.[35] By the close of 1866, the planters were in possession of almost all the Sea Island plantations that had not been sold outright by the Direct Tax Commission.

Life went on, but times were hard for all, including the white planters who had regained their lands. For some of the Negroes whose hopes had been betrayed by restoration, another avenue of purchase opened up in the fall of 1865. Neither in 1864 nor in 1865 had Edward Philbrick made a profit on his cotton crop, and he subsequently returned to Boston. Soon after he arrived in the North, he received a letter from Henry

34. Myrta Lockett Avary, *Dixie After the War* (New York: Doubleday, Page & Co., 1906), pp. 213–14.

35. Although most of Sherman's Field Order had been rescinded, Saxton had executed 5,000 warrants, thereby giving these holders titles to the land. Of these 5,000 warrants only 1,565 were finally validated by the military. Early in 1867 the Negroes had to exchange them for leases on government-owned tax lands in the vicinity of Beaufort, with option to buy twenty-acre plots within six years (Martin Abbott, "The Freedmen's Bureau in South Carolina, 1865–1872," [unpublished Ph.D. dissertation, Dept. of History, Emory University, Atlanta, 1954] pp. 95–99).

Seabrook (a planter on Hilton Head) written in behalf of Captain John Fripp. Fripp's plantations had been among those purchased by Philbrick during the tax sales of March, 1863; now Seabrook sought the return of these lands to their original owner.[36]

Philbrick decided to sell his holdings. Even at that early date, he may have perceived that the planters would sue for the restitution of properties sold outright in the land sales of 1863 and 1864, and he could not presume to know whether or not his own titles would be upheld. Or, perhaps, this was his last blow in defense of his convictions that Negroes could become independent farmers. In any case, he sent a surveyor to divide and sell his land—some to white men and more to Negroes—at $5.00 an acre. This was five times what he had paid per acre in 1863 but less than the current market price.[37]

Five days after the surveyor had been sent to St. Helena, Philbrick wrote Seabrook, but he did not reveal his intentions. "The lands in my possession I hold only as joint proprietor with a number of Northern gentlemen, and although I am authorized to sell these lands on liberal terms, your letter is too indefinite to enter into negotiations at present."[38] Meanwhile, the sales to Negroes and whites had begun.

In this case, the buyers were fortunate. Later, during Reconstruction, when the planters did bring suit for the restitution of their tax-forfeited estates, the court refused to go behind the certificates, and the verdict was in favor of the Negroes.[39]

Nevertheless, elsewhere the revolution on the Sea Islands was rolled back. In 1869, the U. S. Congress restored Pinckney

36. Seabrook to Philbrick, September 30, 1865, James Butler Campbell Papers, S.C.L.
37. Pearson (ed.), p. 315; Rose, p. 310.
38. Philbrick to Seabrook, October 10, 1865, Campbell Papers, S. C. L.
39. Holland (ed.), p. 239; Rose, p. 397; Williamson, p. 86.

Island to the Pinckney heirs,[40] and this action dealt the final blow to the Sea Island experiment in Negro landownership. Except for the freedmen who had benefited from the tax sales on St. Helena and Port Royal, the Negroes' hopes had been betrayed.[41] The Federal government, which had fostered such hopes among the South Carolina freedmen, left them after the war with no possession other than a memory.

In addition, many of the humanitarians who had come to the Sea Islands dedicated to the ideal of remodeling Southern society had become bitterly disillusioned by the end of the war. They complained frequently of the freedmen's ingratitude, unfaithfulness, and many other failings.[42] Most of them returned discouraged to the North. Philbrick summed up the disillusionment of those who had expected miracles when the Negro had been proclaimed free. "The change is too great to be made in a day."[43]

Dreamers and realists alike had failed. But in another sense the abortive Sea Island experiment was not a failure but rather part of a continuing process. It set the South Carolina Negroes apart from other southern Negroes, and out of their short-lived experience in property holding came the determination to acquire land on their own initiative. The social experiment had unleashed forces that would find expression in the Reconstruction Land Commission.

40. 1868 Petition, Pinckney Island, Southern Historical Collection, Chapel Hill, University of North Carolina.

41. Much of this land remained in the hands of the Negroes, and in the 1930's St. Helena Island became the focal point for sociological studies of black yeomanry, including the studies by: Guion Griffis Johnson, *A Social History of the Sea Islands: With Special Reference to St. Helena Island, South Carolina* (Chapel Hill: The University of North Carolina Press, 1930); Guy Benton Johnson, *Folk Culture on St. Helena Island, South Carolina* (Chapel Hill: The University of North Carolina Press, 1930); Thomas Johnson Woofter, *Black Yeomanry: Life on St. Helena Island* (New York: Henry Holt & Company, 1930).

42. Rose, p. 366.

43. Pearson (ed.), p. 317.

2

Though no "promised land" was forthcoming in 1866, Congress in that year did see fit to extend the Homestead Act to include all public property in the Confederate states. The opportunity to acquire 160 acres of surveyed public domain after five years of continuous residence and payment of a small registration fee, or after six months' residence at $1.25 per acre, brought about a notable increase in the number of small farms in the South.[44] But since South Carolina possessed no public land, the freedmen there gained nothing from the extension of the Homestead Act.

Through their own initiative some Negroes purchased land at the prevailing low price, but they were few indeed.[45] Estates offered for sale usually were too large and involved too great an investment for the penniless black man. But for some, relief was to come from an unexpected quarter.

Privations and hardships induced a small number of South Carolina landowners to subdivide their large plantations and sell off the lots to Negroes, since the price they could get for the subdivided tracts was higher than the current market price for land sold in bulk.[46] David Riker of Charleston was one of the first native South Carolinians after the war to sell land to freedmen. Following the procedure set up by the Federal government on St. Helena Island in December, 1863, Riker subdivided his Woodville plantation, on the Wando River, "into small farms from 6 to 18 acres—well drained and planted on each of them is a well-built—comfortable house."[47]

Initially, the venture was successful; 220 Negroes settled

44. Martin Abbott, "Free Land, Free Labor, and The Freedmen's Bureau," *Agricultural History*, XXX (1956), 150–56.
45. Coulter, p. 112; W. E. Burghardt Du Bois, *Black Reconstruction, 1860–1880* (Philadelphia: Albert Saifer, 1935), p. 603; Williamson, p. 142.
46. Anderson *Intelligencer*, September 27, 1867.
47. David Riker to Governor Robert K. Scott, April 25, 1869, Loose Paper File, Governor Scott's Papers, General Letters, April, 1869, S.C.A.

on the 1,300 acres and agreed to pay Riker $12 an acre. Furthermore, the Freedmen's Bureau, looking upon the community with favor, built a schoolhouse at Woodville. The school soon became the hub of the community, serving as a church and social hall as well as an educational center. Within 200 yards of the school was a stone dwelling and stables; the buildings came to house a country store.[48]

Although the land was fertile and the Negroes appeared prosperous, Riker in three years collected only $200 from the settlers. Since five years of war had exhausted his personal resources, Riker could ill afford to carry the Woodville community indefinitely. To avoid selling the plantation at auction, he persuaded his father-in-law Francis Sires to buy the land. The bankrupt Riker went off to Brazil leaving Sires, a prosperous businessman before the war, to carry on the ill-fated experiment.[49] But Sires, old and burdened with debt, soon lost patience with the delinquent settlers and threatened them with eviction if they did not pay all their outstanding debts by January, 1870. The Negroes failed to comply, so he sold the Woodville settlement.[50] The outcome was fortuitous both for Sires and for the Negroes. Sires sold the Woodville plantation to the Land Commission, receiving $8,000, twice his asking price, and the Negroes benefited by the reduction in price from $12 to $3 an acre with payments spread over eight years.[51]

Although the Woodville community had been dictated by economic necessity—a financial scheme to improve Riker's waning fortune—some evidence of *noblesse oblige* was ap-

48. *Ibid.*
49. *Ibid.*; *Reports and Resolutions of the General Assembly of the State of South Carolina, 1872–1873* (Columbia: Republican Printing Company, 1872), pp. 143–44, cited hereafter as *Repts. and Resols.*
50. *Ibid.*; Purchase Book, Land Commissioners' Office, p. 29, S.C.A.
51. *Ibid.*; Riker to Scott April 25, 1869; Accounts of Sales A, Secretary of State's Office, p. 19, S.C.A.; *Repts. and Resols., 1871–1872*, pp. 340–41.

parent in both Riker's and Sires' concern for the well-being of the freedmen. Sires had been persuaded to purchase Woodville "for the purpose of protecting the settlers and allowing them a year or two more to discharge the debt." Furthermore, when Sires decided to dispose of Woodville, the settlement was offered to the state because Riker, the original owner, would be "very sorry to see the place purchased by a stranger, and they driven from a spot to which they are so much attached."[52] Most native white planters, however, could not afford to resume the ante-bellum role of paternalism. They were reluctant to sell their lands to former slaves because of the risk and expense it entailed. Few Negroes could purchase an entire estate, sub-dividing was costly, and the reliability of the Negroes in meeting their obligations was uncertain. The reluctance to sell to freedmen does not appear to have stemmed from fear of Negro equality through ownership of land; it simply made more sense to the owners, especially in the light of the Woodville failure, to sell their holdings in bulk to Northern speculators.

Since the Federal government demonstrated it would not, and the majority of native planters could not even if they chose to, help the freedmen obtain land, an alternative was for the Negroes themselves to combine their resources and their labor in their quest for homesteads. A few did make such an effort.

Several cooperatives were formed in the low country, especially in Charleston and Colleton counties where there were concentrations of Negroes. The associations were composed principally of freedmen who worked for hire. Dues were collected; when sufficient capital had been accumulated the members of the society selected a plantation and began the payments, usually spread over a three-year period. The land was distributed equally among the members of the society; each

52. Riker to Scott, September 23, 1869, S.C.A.

member was free to work as it suited him and could dispose
of his crop as he deemed proper. All that was required of a
member was the prompt payment of his dues.[53]

One such operation in the low country was described to the
delegates at the South Carolina Constitutional Convention:

> About one hundred poor colored men of Charleston met
> together and formed themselves into a Charleston Land Com-
> pany. They subscribed for a number of shares at $10 per
> share, one dollar payable monthly. They have been meeting
> for a year. Yesterday [January 23, 1868] they purchased 600
> acres of land for $6,600 that would have sold for $25,000 or
> $50,000 in better times.[54]

The Atlantic Land Company was another such Negro association established in Charleston County. In 1868, the members purchased a tract of land—Bull's Island—near the city for
$15,000. The cooperative foundered when the last $6,000
owed on the investment could not be raised, and in 1870 proceedings of foreclosure were instituted. Edward Lee, secretary
and treasurer of the Atlantic Land Company, appealed to
Governor Robert Scott, a Republican, for assistance. According to Lee, the Charlestonians refused to lend the members
the money because they were both Republicans and black
men; hence Scott, as the most "prominent member of the Republican party . . . . must save them from a sale of their property."[55] Furthermore, Lee threatened that unless something
were done at once in behalf of the cooperative, the members—
he included a petition signed by eighty of them—would bring

53. *New York Times*, August 17, 1873; New York *Tribune*, June 30, 1869;
Charleston *News and Courier*, August 13, 1873.

54. *Proceedings of the Constitutional Convention of South Carolina, 1868*
(2 vols., Charleston: Denny & Co., 1868), I, p. 117; cited hereafter as *Proceedings*.

55. Two enclosures: Edward W. Lee to Governor Robert K. Scott, February
18, 1870; Lee to C. P. Leslie, February 18, 1870; Loose Paper File, Governor
Scott's Papers, General Letters, February–March 1870, S.C.A.

political pressure to bear upon their representatives.[56] But since no deed is recorded as having been issued to the cooperative, we may assume that the Atlantic Land Company disappeared from existence. In 1872, another association reportedly bought a 750-acre plantation on Edisto Island. It is unlikely, however, that after the war many freedmen acquired land through cooperative purchase.[57]

It seemed that large-scale Negro ownership of the soil could not be achieved through individuals acting independently, nor through group action on the part of poor black men. For success, a broader, more unified program had to be adopted. The Negroes possessed the potential leadership; such a program of ownership obviously would attract many followers. All that was lacking was the opportunity to assemble in a body and discuss the most feasible course of action to bring it about. The opportunity came at the Constitutional Convention of 1868.

When the "convention of the people of South Carolina" convened on January 14, 1868, 76 of the 124 delegates were Negroes.[58] They were thus in an excellent position to exert pressure for land reforms. At first they hesitated, being initially inclined to turn once again to the Federal government. Richard H. Cain, the convention's leading spokesman for land reform, was a Virginia-born free mulatto who had been sent to South Carolina by the African Methodist Episcopal Church at the end of the war. At the time of the convention he was minister of the Emmanuel A. M. E. Church on Calhoun Street in Charleston and editor of the Negro newspaper, the *Mission-*

---

56. Atlantic Land Company Petition to C. P. Leslie, February 18, 1870, Governor Scott's Papers.

57. Williamson, p. 156.

58. Francis Butler Simkins and Robert Hillard Woody, *South Carolina During Reconstruction* (Chapel Hill: The University of North Carolina Press, 1932), pp. 90–91.

ary Record.[59] The Reverend Cain, a powerful leader of the Negroes in Charleston, proposed a resolution to the convention to petition Congress for a million dollars to purchase land for the freedmen of South Carolina.[60]

Though most of the delegates supported Cain's resolution, Charles P. Leslie, a white "carpetbag" delegate from Barnwell, went on record as opposing it. Leslie charged that the resolution was a political ruse to trick the Negro and gain his vote and that he, Leslie, would not be made a fool of by a stunt that Congress was sure to repudiate.[61] A New York *Tribune* reporter covering the convention "seconded" Leslie's opposition. In an article opposing Federal aid, he wrote that Negroes should "root hog or die." Cain, of course, was indignant. "In the meantime," Cain retorted, "we ought to have some place to root. My proposition is simply to give the hog some place to root."[62] Furthermore, he explained, the million dollars was not to be construed as an outright gift; it was to be a government loan which the Negroes would pay back within five years.[63] Once the resolution had been clarified, many white delegates came to support a petition to Congress for the loan.

Among the white delegates who went on record in support of Cain's resolution were Christopher Columbus Bowen, Daniel H. Chamberlain, Franklin J. Moses, Jr., and Niles G. Parker. All were leading figures in Radical Reconstruction. Bowen, one of the foremost Republican lawyers in the state and an organizer of the Republican party, and Chamberlain, soon to become Scott's attorney general and in 1874 to be elected gov-

59. *Biographical Dictionary of the American Congress, 1774–1949* (Washington, 1950), p. 954; William J. Simmons, *Men of Mark: Eminent, Progressive and Rising* (Cleveland, Ohio: George M. Rewell & Co., 1887), pp. 866–67; Williamson, p. 190.

60. *Proceedings*, I, p. 360.

61. *Ibid.*, pp. 376–78.

62. New York *Tribune*, February 14, 1868; *Proceedings*, I, p. 379.

63. *Ibid.*, pp. 379–82.

ernor of South Carolina, endorsed the resolution on the grounds that the loyal Negro Republican majority was entitled to economic relief.[64] Franklin J. Moses, Jr., a native South Carolinian who was to be elected governor in 1872, stated in support of the petition that land would make citizens of the freedmen and "bind them to the Government with ties that can never be broken."[65] Niles G. Parker, elected state treasurer in 1868, expressed some reservations. "I am opposed to legislating for a class," he said, though he added that if the resolution were amended to ask Congress for money to buy homesteads for not only the colored but for all the poor, he would vote for it.[66]

When the yeas and nays were demanded, it was a resounding victory for Cain's resolution—101 for, five against.[67] Besides Leslie, only one other white delegate, Reuben Holmes of Beaufort, a washing-machine salesman in Boston before the war, voted against the petition.[68] Three Negro delegates, Robert Smalls, Stephen A. Swails, and William J. Whipper, cast negative votes. Smalls, a native-born Negro who had been impressed into Confederate service as the pilot of the harbor steamer *Planter*, had become a hero by escaping into the lines of the Federal squadron, using the ship itself for his transportation. Swails and Whipper had come to the state as soldiers and remained to work in the Freedmen's Bureau.[69] They voted

64. *Ibid.*, pp. 410–13.
65. *Ibid.*, p. 434.
66. *Ibid.*, pp. 409–11.
67. *Ibid.*, p. 439.
68. *Ibid.*; Reuben G. Holmes Papers, *passim*, S.C.L. Surprisingly enough, Holmes was to be the delegate who presented to the convention the ordinance embodying the concept of the Land Commission (*Proceedings*, p. 507).
69. Emily B. Reynolds and Joan Reynolds Faunt (eds.), *Biographical Directory of the Senate of the State of South Carolina, 1776–1964* (Columbia: South Carolina Archives Department, 1964), pp. 310, 318; Williamson, pp. 30, 330–31.

against the measure because they thought it "raised the hopes of the entire poor people of the country, and the freedmen would leave their contracts, run to land offices where three quarters will go away with shattered hopes."[70] Furthermore, Whipper declared, "the sooner every man knows that to acquire land he must earn it . . . the better."[71] Their pessimism was not shared by the others. To most of the delegates the knotty problem of Negro landownership had been easily resolved in just five days of running debate.

This optimism, however, was quickly dispelled by a telegram from Senator Henry Wilson of Massachusetts. Wilson told the convention to drop the resolution because the petition would be defeated in Congress.[72]

After deliberation, the delegates agreed upon a substitute bill. An ordinance embodied in the Constitution of 1868 provided for the creation of a state land commission. The State of South Carolina, not the Federal government, was to be the agent through which the landless could acquire homesteads. Too similar to be coincidental, the ordinance setting up the state agency apparently had been patterned after the national Homestead Act of 1862, superimposed by the delegates upon a single state. The delegates left the following instructions for the next session of the South Carolina legislature, 1868–1869:

> Section 1. . . . provide for the establishing of a Board to be known as and designated as Commissioners of Public Lands. . . .
> Section 2. The Commissioners of Public Lands shall have authority, under regulations provided by law, to purchase at public sales, improved and unimproved real estate within

70. *Proceedings*, I, p. 401.
71. *Ibid.*, p. 402.
72. *Ibid.*, pp. 438–39.

this state, which in the judgment of such Commissioners shall be suitable for the purposes intended by the fourth section of this Article; *Provided* that the aggregate amount of purchases made in any fiscal year shall not exceed the par value of the public stock of this State created and appropriated by the Legislature for the purposes contemplated in the fourth section of this Article . . . .

Section 3. The Legislature shall have authority to issue to said Commissioners public stock of this state to such amount as it may deem expedient; which stock, or the proceeds thereof, the Commissioners shall have authority to apply in payment of all purchases made in accordance with the second section of this Article . . . .

Section 4. The said Commissioners shall have authority under such regulations as shall be established by the Legislature, to cause the said lands to be surveyed and laid off in suitable tracts to be sold to actual settlers, subject to the condition that one half thereof shall be placed under cultivation within three years from the date of any such purchase. And that the purchaser thereof shall annually pay interest upon the amount of such purchase money remaining unpaid, at the rate of 7 per cent per annum; and also all taxes imposed thereon by or under the authority of the United States or of this State, and in addition thereto, shall, in every year after the third from the date of said purchase, pay such proportion of the principal of said purchase as shall be required by the Legislature. The titles to said lands shall remain in the State until the amount of said purchase shall be issued to the purchaser, which shall be assignable after three years from the date thereof.

Section 5. All lands purchased by said Commissioners or the proceeds of the sales thereof, shall be and remain pledged for the redemption of the public stock issued under section three of this Article; but the Legislature shall have authority, subject to such lien and pledge, to make upon the faith and credit of such fund, further issues of public stock . . . .

Section 6. The Legislature shall provide by law for the security of the funds in the hands of the Commissioners of

Public Lands, and for the accountability of such officers, and shall require bonds to be given therefor.[73]

When the opportunity had come to satisfy their land hunger, the Negro majority at the Constitutional Convention had acted. A single Southern state was about to undertake an unprecedented step in the direction of land reform.[74]

73. *Ibid.,* pp. 508–09.

74. Land division through heavy taxation was discussed at the convention and is viewed by Joel Williamson as an alternative to the Land Commission for bringing about land redistribution (For an account of the Republican tax program, *see*: Williamson, pp. 148–59). The delegates, anticipating such a tax program once the Republicans were in power on the state level, adopted measures which were to supplement the program. One provided for a uniform rate of assessment of all property based on actual value. The new system was a radical departure from the ante-bellum system of taxing land and slaves lightly while the mercantile interests bore the brunt of taxation (Simkins and Woody, p. 177). Other measures adopted by the convention included a stay law designed to delay forced sales, allegedly to allow the landless time to acquire capital to purchase land and to allow the new tax rates to depress land prices (*Proceedings*, pp. 113–48, *passim*; Williamson, p. 150). Moreover, once the agriculturist acquired a small farm he was protected from loss of his property through civil action by a constitutional provision that exempted from such sales a homestead worth $1,000 and personal property to the value of $500 (*Proceedings*, pp. 882, 888–89).

With the advent of the Republican state government, the new tax program was inaugurated. At first the program was conceived of as a heavy tax upon unused land. Later, however, the concept of heavy taxes was expanded to include not only unused lands, but all property, real and personal (Williamson, p. 148). Although the state tax was reportedly no higher than in some Northern states, in addition to the state tax, each county taxed its property owners, and a school tax was often quoted separately (*Ibid.*, pp. 150–51). As a result tax bills were so high that vast quantities of land were forfeited to the state annually. Though South Carolina Negroes did take advantage of these conditions to acquire homesteads by purchasing forfeited lands, once they had become property owners they were subject to the same adverse effects of the Republican tax program as white South Carolinians. Negroes as well as whites forfeited their lands for taxes during Reconstruction (Charleston *News and Courier*, August 13, 1873; Williamson, p. 156). When the Redeemers regained power, the Republican tax program was repudiated, and many whites whose property had been forfeited to the state had their land restored to the tax rolls and were given liberal time limits within which to pay off their deficiencies (*Repts. and Resols., 1877–1878*, p. vi; Williamson, p. 159).

CHAPTER II

"Homes for the Homeless and Land for the Landless"

SOUTH CAROLINA'S CONSTITUTION of 1868, the handiwork of a convention composed of "carpetbaggers," "scalawags," and Negroes, has been described as follows:

> The learning of the leaders bore fruit in a constitution written in excellent English and embodying some of the best legal principles of the age. In letter it was as good as any other constitution the state has ever had, or as most American states had at that time. This assertion is supported by the practical endorsement which a subsequent generation of South Carolinians gave it; the Conservative whites were content to live under it for eighteen years after they recovered control of the state government, and when in 1895 they met to make a new constitution, the document they produced had many of the features of the constitution of 1868.[1]

Although the constitution had all the earmarks of theoretical merit, the majority of whites condemned it as being repugnant to the state's traditions. Moreover, they repudiated the

---

1. Simkins and Woody, pp. 93–94.

idea of having legislation enacted by their former slaves. In an effort to block ratification of the constitution and stem the tide of Republicanism, the Democrats in the spring of 1868 campaigned to make known their protest against the Constitution of 1868 "on account of the usurped and polluted source from whence it springs. . . . It must remain in all time to come a badge of South Carolina's dishonor and degradation and especially the dishonor of anyone who votes for its ratification."[2] Since many of the state's prominent citizens had been disfranchised, only by enlisting the support of the Negroes could the Democrats hope to block both the ratification of the Constitution and the election of Republican nominees to state offices. Prominent leaders such as James L. Orr and Wade Hampton again made earnest addresses to Negro audiences to vote with the conservative whites. Yet the Democrats once more failed to breathe life into their organization and failed to win over the Negroes. In the April elections the Constitution was ratified by a vote of 70,758 to 27,228, and a "carpetbagger," Robert K. Scott of Napoleon, Ohio, became the first Republican governor of South Carolina. With his victory the Republican party seemed firmly entrenched. In the general assembly only 6 of the 31 senators and 14 of the 124 representatives were Democrats.[3]

The plight of the Democrats seemed hopeless, but, surprisingly enough, in the elections for county officers held in June, 1868, many Democrats were elected. Records available for 16 counties, approximately half of the counties in the state, indicate that 61 of 119 office holders elected in June, 1868 were unable to subscribe to the test oath of 1862, which required one to swear that he had never voluntarily aided or

2. Anderson *Intelligencer*, April 22, 1868.

3. Simkins and Woody, p. 109. Moreover, Negroes outnumbered whites in the lower house of the general assembly throughout Reconstruction.

supported the Confederacy.[4] In other counties the same circumstances prevailed.[5] Perhaps it was this turn of events that encouraged native white leaders to try once again to win Negro votes for the national elections in November.

In August, Wade Hampton addressed a Greenville Democratic Club meeting. He told the freedmen to put their trust in their old friends and repudiate the Republicans, who sought only to dupe them. In illustrating Republican deceit, he alluded to the proposed Land Commission Act. "The Radicals don't want you, if you have no money," Hampton told his up-country audience. "I have heard of forty acres of land, but have never seen it. A piece of earth six feet long and three feet wide is all they will ever give you."[6] The Democratic campaign, however, failed before it was well underway. When early Republican victories in the North and West were reported in October, most native whites conceded defeat and withdrew from active politics.[7] The success of the Republicans soon brought about legislation for the relief of the Negro majority.

The State House of Representatives quickly passed the bill

4. MS E. W. Everson to Robert K. Scott, June 22, 1868, Bureau of Refugees, Freedmen and Abandoned Land Records, The National Archives, Washington, D.C., cited in Martin Abbott, "County Officers in South Carolina in 1868," *South Carolina Historical Magazine*, LX (January, 1959), 30–40. The Everson manuscript is a synopsis of reports submitted by agents of the Freedmen's Bureau in response to a directive from Scott.

5. Governor Scott's Papers contain numerous letters from ex-Confederates elected to county offices who were seeking to have their disabilities removed so they could assume office. *See*: W. H. Langston to R. K. Scott, July 3, 1868; John H. Goodwin to Scott, July 6, 1868; John W. Burbridge to Scott, July 7, 1868; William McDaniel, Alexander McBee, and H. M. Smith to Scott, July 8, 1868; Dr. R. H. Edmonds to Scott, July 13, 1868; James Hemphill to Scott, July 17, 1868; William N. Mount to Scott, July 25, 1868; and folders 31, 33, *passim*, Governor Scott's Papers, S.C.A.

6. Greenville *Southern Enterprise*, August 19, 1868.

7. Anderson *Intelligencer*, October 11, 1868; Williamson, pp. 351–53; William H. Trescot to Henry S. Sanford, October 21, 1868, Henry Shelton Sanford Papers, General Sanford Memorial Library, Sanford, Florida.

establishing the South Carolina Land Commission, essentially
as conceived by the convention. In the Senate, Richard Cain
(sponsor of the original convention resolution) and other
Negro senators pressed for immediate passage of the bill but
met with delay. Not until March 27, 1869, one year after the
convention had adopted the Land Commission ordinance, did
the legislature establish the state agency and provide for the
appointment of a land commissioner.[8]

The act provided for the establishment of an Advisory
Board composed of the five most important state officials: the
governor, the secretary of state, the treasurer, the attorney general, and the comptroller general. They were to direct the
newly created agency and to appoint a land commissioner who
was to be governed by their instruction and advice.[9]

It was the duty of the land commissioner to purchase plantations for the state, to employ surveyors to subdivide the
tracts into sections containing no less than 25 acres nor more
than 100 acres, and to sell these lots to actual settlers. During
the first three years of occupancy the settlers were to pay the
land taxes and 6 per cent interest yearly on the principal of
the loan. Speculators were excluded by a provision in the act
requiring half of each tract to be placed under cultivation
within five years of the date of purchase. After three years of
continuous residence and compliance with all the stated requirements, the settlers were to receive certificates of purchase
and begin payments on the purchase price. The title to the
land, however, was to remain with the state until the full

8. *Journal of the House of Representatives of the General Assembly of the
State of South Carolina* (1868, regular session), p. 425, cited hereafter as *House
Journal*; *Journal of the Senate of the General Assembly of the State of South
Carolina* (1868–1869, regular session), p. 542, cited hereafter as *Senate Journal*;
Statutes at Large of the State of South Carolina (Columbia, 1836–), XIV, pp.
275–77, cited hereafter as *Statutes at Large*.

9. *Ibid.*, pp. 275–76.

amount—principal plus 6 per cent interest—had been paid. The settlers were required to complete their time payments within eight years after receiving certificates.[10]

For this praiseworthy purpose, $200,000 in bonds were authorized by the legislature to be issued for the commission's purchases; the bonds were placed in the hands of the state treasurer, and by him in the hands of a financial agent in New York for negotiation. The secretary of the treasury was to pay for the lands with the funds raised through the sale of the state bonds by the New York agent, H. H. Kimpton.[11] A larger appropriation of $500,000 was made in 1870.

White reaction to the passage of the Land Commission Act was mixed, but most conservatives failed to grasp the significance of this pioneer reform bill. In general, the anti-administration newspapers adopted a "wait and see" policy reserving decision until the results of the land redistribution program could be ascertained. However, the editor of the Winnsboro News registered strong disapproval. "We do deny that any good can come of a state government leveling its credit," he declared, "for the purpose of creating land-owners out of land-laborers, than for the purpose of creating house-owners out of house-tenants, or ship-owners out of sailors, or store-owners out of clerks. . . ." He urged the legislature to repeal the bill and readopt a policy of laissez-faire so that the situation could regulate itself. "It is a mischievious meddling and an impertinent interference—a job, and an expensive one," he warned.[12]

Although white landowners were generally quiescent, Jacob Schirmer, a Charleston planter, failing to distinguish between

10. Ibid., p. 276. Six per cent interest was low in comparison with the high rates of interest, ranging from 12 to 36 per cent, which prevailed in South Carolina during Reconstruction (Williamson, p. 174).

11. Ibid.

12. Winnsboro News, September 8, 1869.

good and bad Republican legislation, attacked it all: "The legislature now in session [1869] is passing laws that are all obnoxious to the law abiding citizens, and you can perceive in almost every act—the governing principle of self-interest directing them and every act to be done for the good of the State or City generally can only be done by extensive Bribery and corruption in the lobby of Legislature Hall."[13]

Perhaps the most significant indictment of the act was the refusal of the poor whites to participate in the land experiment. Although, under the act, state-owned tracts were to be sold at nominal cost to the poor of both races, the Negro from its inception dominated the program. Most poor whites preferred to shun any close social or economic association with the former slaves (*See* Appendix II). By voluntarily excluding themselves from living side by side with the blacks, they probably assumed they were maintaining their "superiority" over them.

Soon after the passage of the Land Commission Act, the Advisory Board met in Governor Scott's office. At this first session the governor recommended the appointment of his friend Charles P. Leslie as land commissioner.[14] The Anderson *Intelligencer*, commenting on the board's approval of Leslie, charged that his "appointment is doubtless made to soothe the 'irrepressible's' feelings in consequence of his losing the United States Marshallship for this state."[15]

Since the success of any undertaking, large or small, is dependent upon the character of the personnel who compose its organization, it is necessary to inquire into the composition of the Land Commission. The six men, Scott, Chamberlain,

13. MSS Diary of Jacob L. Schirmer, I, December, 1869, South Carolina Historical Society, Charleston.

14. MS Affidavit of Niles G. Parker, January 23, 1878, Samuel Dibble Papers, Duke University, Durham.

15. April 22, 1869.

Parker, Neagle, Cardozo, and Leslie, were among the dominating personalities in the Reconstruction period, but as far as the native whites could determine, the Advisory Board members and the land commissioner left much to be desired. Five were "carpetbaggers" and one was a Charleston Negro.

Charles P. Leslie, the first land commissioner, had served in the New York legislature before the war. In 1865 he left Brooklyn and moved to South Carolina—one of the many "carpetbaggers" who came South for the sole purpose of entering politics. Leslie was successively a U. S. revenue agent, delegate to the state constitutional convention in 1868, and state senator from Barnwell County.[16] Loquacious in the legislature, often held spellbound by his own rhetoric, Leslie made himself known far beyond what his capabilities should have warranted. He alienated his colleagues by his vacillations on controversial issues and by his grandstand displays in the Senate. A year before his appointment as land commissioner, Leslie had been ruled out of order by the president *pro tempore*. Contemptuously Leslie replied, "You may gag me and rush things through as you please, you will be sorry for it." Contempt was the charge lodged against him, and he was suspended from the Senate.[17] On apologizing to the Senate, the senator from Barnwell had been permitted to resume his seat. Nevertheless, he remained a controversial figure, accusing and accused, throughout the Reconstruction era.

Robert K. Scott, Republican governor of South Carolina 1868–1872, was a native of Pennsylvania who had migrated to Ohio and then to California, returning to Napoleon, Ohio,

16. *Biographical Dictionary of the S. C. Senate*, p. 257; Camden (S.C.) *Journal*, June 17, 1869; Simkins and Woody, p. 93.

17. Papers Relating to the Impeachment of Senator Charles P. Leslie, Barnwell County, September 18, 1868, Impeachments 1868, Loose Paper File, S.C.A.; C. P. Leslie to Robert K. Scott, October 16, 1868, Governor Scott's Papers.

before the war. There he was moderately successful as a physician, realtor, and merchant. During the war he was the organizer and colonel of a regiment of Ohio volunteers. In 1866 Scott was appointed assistant commissioner of the Freedmen's Bureau for South Carolina, holding the office until he was inaugurated governor. It was Scott who replaced Rufus Saxton in 1866 and carried out, with the help of regular military forces, the removal of the Negroes and the restoration of the Sea Island plantations to their original owners.[18] In 1869, his capabilities as chief executive still were untested. By his past actions he did not appear to be a friend of the Negro, but merely by being the leader of the Republican party he made himself and his motives suspect to the Democratic electorate.[19]

The genial Niles G. Parker, state treasurer during Scott's two administrations, was said to have been before the war the unsuccessful owner of a restaurant and bar in Haverhill, Massachusetts.[20] This hardly qualified him to handle all the financial transactions of a state. Coming to South Carolina as captain in a regiment of Negro volunteers, he settled in Charleston as a planter and merchant. In 1867, General Canby appointed Parker an alderman for the city of Charleston. Elected a member of the Constitutional Convention, he was made chairman of the Committee on Finance. So successful was he in raising the necessary expenses of the convention that his name was put in nomination for state treasurer.[21]

John L. Neagle, comptroller general, was a native of North Carolina. During the war he served as an assistant surgeon in

18. Rose, pp. 356–57; Williamson, p. 84.
19. Simkins and Woody, p. 113. Martin Abbott's book on the South Carolina Freedmen's Bureau contains a very favorable account of Scott's actions as assistant commissioner of the bureau.
20. Anderson *Intelligencer*, June 28, 1870.
21. Orangeburg *News and Times*, September 22, 1877; Simkins and Woody, p. 114.

the Confederate Army. Later he settled in Rock Hill, South Carolina, where he kept a store, and in 1868 he was sent as a delegate from York County to the Constitutional Convention.[22]

Daniel Henry Chamberlain, one of the most complex Reconstruction figures, was attorney general during Scott's two administrations. A native of Massachusetts, educated at Yale, Amherst, and Harvard, Chamberlain was probably the best educated public official of the period. He first came to South Carolina as a planter and then became a politician.[23] He is best known as the reform governor of South Carolina during the last two years of Republican rule. Since his campaign for re-election to the governorship in 1876, he has been the subject of bitter controversy by those attacking or defending his sincerity as a reformer. In his capacity as chief executive he appears to have been a reformer,[24] but there may be some question as to whether Chamberlain refrained from using the office of attorney general for personal profit. From 1870 through 1872 he was a member of the Greenville and Columbia railroad ring; he admitted later that he dreamed of making thousands on the venture.[25] Moreover his transactions with H. H. Kimpton, the financial agent of the state, and his actions in regard to the Land Commission are also open to question.[26] It is certain that he could not have been oblivious to the corruption which surrounded him, but perhaps it was as he confided to a friend in 1875: "My evils have heretofore come

22. *Ibid.*, pp. 114–15.

23. Charleston *News*, March 9, 1868; Charleston *News and Courier*, May 22, 1877; Simkins and Woody, pp. 115–16.

24. Walter Allen, *Governor Chamberlain's Administration in South Carolina* (New York: Putnam, 1888), *passim*; Williamson, pp. 400–06.

25. D. H. Chamberlain to F. W. Dawson, June 9, 1875, F. W. Dawson Papers, Duke University; *Repts. and Resols., 1877–1878*, pp. 1576–81.

26. *See* Chapter III.

from the friendship of bad men. Perhaps I shall fare better if I now have their hatred. At any rate I'm ready to try it."[27]

Francis L. Cardozo, the only Negro on the Advisory Board, was a free-born mulatto from Charleston. He, too, was far better educated than his Republican colleagues. He had attended an ante-bellum school for Negroes in the city, and had completed his formal training at the University of Glasgow. After three more years of formal preparation for the ministry at Presbyterian seminaries in Edinburgh and London, he went to New Haven to accept a pulpit. After the war he returned to his native state and entered politics. He was the most prominent Negro to hold office in South Carolina, serving as secretary of state under Scott 1868–1872, and treasurer under Moses and Chamberlain 1872–1876.[28] While acting as a member of the Advisory Board, Cardozo strove to safeguard the interests of his race. Nevertheless, at a crucial moment in the operation of the Land Commission, Cardozo quit his post.[29]

Thus it can be seen that in the early stages of the Land Commission experiment most native whites probably had cause to wonder whether the Advisory Board members considered themselves *bona fide* representatives of the state, dispensers of charity, or opportunists in search of personal aggrandizement. Time would tell.

It was not until five months after the passage of the act that the land commissioner was finally ready to proceed with the experiment. In August, 1869, Leslie published a notice in-

27. D. H. Chamberlain to F. W. Dawson, May 11, 1875, F. W. Dawson Papers, cited in Williamson, p. 404.

28. Edward F. Sweat, "Francis L. Cardozo, Profile of Integrity in Reconstruction Politics," *Journal of Negro History*, XLVI (January, 1961), 218; Simmons, pp. 428–31.

29. MS Proceedings of the Advisory Board, Minutes October 6, 1869–April 1, 1872, October 30, 1869, S.C.A., cited hereafter as Advisory Board Minutes.

viting all persons owning desirable land, wishing to sell it, and willing to accept market prices to forward their proposals to the Land Commission.[30] Standard applications provided by the commission were to be submitted.[31] At Advisory Board meetings, Leslie submitted the applications to the board members. Although the commissioner could make recommendations, all authority to purchase rested with the Advisory Board. The assent of any three, either in regular session or individually in private, determined the purchases to be made. When a majority had approved, Leslie submitted the titles to the attorney general. After Chamberlain had investigated the owner's title and declared it valid, the state treasurer was instructed to purchase the plantation.[32]

What prompted South Carolinians to submit applications to sell their plantations, thereby indirectly giving support to the express purposes and goals of the South Carolina Land Commission? The depression, the dislocation in agriculture, the devastation of the low country, the neglect of agriculture in many places for the entire duration of the war—all were responsible for making Leslie's notice appealing to even the staunchest ex-Confederate. General Matthew C. Butler had come out of the war "twenty-nine years old, with one leg gone, a wife and three children to support, seventy emancipated slaves, a debt of $15,000, and in his pocket $1.75."[33] Butler submitted his application offering to sell 650 acres of his Edgefield plantation to the Land Commission at ten dollars

30. Executive Department, Land Commissioner's Office, Bulletin, August 11, 1869, Loose Papers, S.C.A.

31. Samples of Land Commission Questionnaires are scattered among the Loose Papers, Land Transfer File, 1866–1877, S.C.A.

32. Repts. and Resols., 1871–1872, pp. 1021, 1023, 1024; Statutes at Large, XIV, pp. 275–77.

33. Avary, pp. 160–61.

an acre.[34] His application was rejected.[35] Other planters by-
passed the formality of the Land Commission's printed questionnaires and applications and appealed directly to Scott or
Leslie, or both. The Land Transfer File is filled with personal letters; some petitioners pleaded for economic relief
through the sale of their plantations, others expressed humanitarian motives or sentiments of *noblesse oblige* as the explanation for their desire to participate in the experiment.

Oliver Farnum, an Orangeburg planter, wrote to Scott pro-
posing to sell 5,000 acres to the state, because his sixteen tenants were in need of homesteads. Farnum wanted to know
whether "the State has the means, and if so, to ask your influence in aiding them to make the purchase. . . . I would very
willingly sell them the land on credit, but am unable to do
so, as I owe a mortgage on the place of $4,000. . . ."[36] Since
mortgaged land was unacceptable for purchase, Farnum's offer
was rejected.

A planter in Lancaster, disclaiming any pecuniary motives,
wrote the governor that the freedmen had asked him to use
his influence in getting them a settlement on his Cedar Creek
plantation. He sought to persuade Scott to purchase his 2,936-
acre plantation. "These Lands are for Sale at a reduced price
our freedmen are anxius [sic] to buy and I believe they will
pay for them by getting them on time as the state proposes."[37]

An eloquent letter addressed to Scott epitomized the high-

34. M. C. Butler to C. P. Leslie, January, 1870, Loose Papers, Land Transfer
File, 1866–1877, Questionnaire.

35. *Ibid.*, notation "rejection" written on Butler's application.

36. Oliver Farnum to Robert Scott, December 3, 1870, Loose Papers, Land
Transfer File, 1866–1877.

37. D. W. Brown to Governor Robert K. Scott, April 29, 1870, *Ibid. See also*:
A. M. Folger to Gov. Scott, May 5, 1870; I. Fraser Matthews to Robert Scott,
January 9, 1870; Mrs. S. S. Cook to R. K. Scott, September 21, 1869; I. I.
Pickens to Gov. Scott, March 3, 1871; Henry Behling to R. C. De Large, April
7, 1870; R. S. G. Appleby to R. K. Scott, June 7, 1870 (*Ibid.*).

est ideals for which the Land Commission had been instituted to serve. A Presbyterian minister, A. D. Francisco, wrote the governor concerning the Negro settlement he had established at Winnsboro, South Carolina. "We have had two schools in the country of 70 and 80 scholars during the summer, besides . . . our school in W.[innsboro] last year numbered 225 scholars. . . . We have also two churches with large sabb[ath] schools in the country." Francisco was worried over the future of his Negro community; it would wither and die, he feared, unless the Land Commission purchased the property. He assured the governor that five Negro men of Winnsboro stood ready to take and to pay for the 355 acres in compliance with the recent law. If the Winnsboro land were to be purchased by the state and resold to the Negroes on easy terms, the houses on the property could be utilized temporarily as a church and a school by his flock, and in addition, five families would be provided with homesteads.[38] Apparently Scott and the commission rejected Francisco's appeal for the survival of the Negro settlement at Winnsboro and his request for homesteads on behalf of the homeless, since no deed is reported. Perhaps the purchase he requested was too insignificant in size. The purpose of the experiment—to settle thousands of Negro families on the land—would have been defeated if the commission's energy had been sapped in handling individual petitions for welfare. The theory of large-scale land redistribution could be accomplished only through the breakup of large landholdings. Unfortunately, a clearcut statement of policy to this effect had not been formulated, hence the land commissioner was forced to scan hundreds of applications offering small farms for sale, thereby delaying the progress of the board.

38. A. D. Francisco to Governor Robert Scott, October 30, 1869, Governor Scott's Papers.

In addition to the letters of planters and philanthropists, many Negroes themselves wrote to the land commissioner pressing him to purchase plantations for them. Since they possessed the necessary votes to keep the state Republican, they dispensed with all the homilies and abstract ideals, and went directly to the heart of the matter. They threatened to withdraw their political support unless land were made available to them. On Edisto Island, a mass meeting of black people convened for the purpose of addressing a petition to Governor Scott in regard to purchasing a 900-acre plantation on that island. Their chairman, James Hutchinson, wrote Scott, "We need this land, and wish you or anyone you can refer us to, to purchase it for us and in due time according to any reasonable regulation . . . we'll refund the money." Hutchinson further informed the governor, "We have stood by and supported you throughout this last campaign almost to a man. . . . We would not have done so had we not believed you were a gentleman of principle having the good of the poorer classes in view as well as that of the rich."[39] Nevertheless, the governor was warned that if he failed to support the Edisto Island petition the Negroes would lose confidence in the governor and withdraw their political support from his administration.[40]

In person, from Lawtonville, in Beaufort County, came a Negro delegation. They asked Scott to use his influence with

39. James Hutchinson to Governor Robert Scott, December 3, 1870, Governor Scott's Papers.

40. *Ibid.* Although no evidence exists that Scott supported the Edisto Island petition, James Hutchinson, the chairman, continued to work for the Republican party. C. C. Bowen in his letter to Chamberlain concerning Negro appointments to political office in Charleston County stated, "Jim Hutchinson of Edisto you know, gratitude prompts his recommendation and demands his appointment" (Bowen to Chamberlain, February 3, 1875, Governor Chamberlain's Papers, S.C.A.). Hutchinson was appointed a Trial Justice (Chamberlain Appointments, 1875, S.C.A.).

the board in purchasing 2,900 acres of cultivated land upon which were 20 well-constructed houses.[41]

Although the legislature had established the commission to provide land for the freedmen at nominal cost, thereby attempting to alleviate their extreme poverty, the commission was to be used by the party to promote political ends. From the onset of Radical Reconstruction, Democrats had grasped the political significance of land. One powerful weapon used by the planters to punish Negroes voting the Radical state ticket had been to eject them from their land. The blacks appealed to the Republican administration to redress the wrongs done them. One Ridgeway Negro, Ishmael Powel, wrote Scott that in his community Democrats had turned them off the land because they had voted the Republican ticket. "Colonel H. C. Davis has ordered several of his labor to leave his houses and we wants [sic] to know from you what we must do. . . ."[42]

The report of Republican Thomas Slider substantiated Powel's complaint and added that in Newberry the Democratic party had made a concerted effort to prevent the sale of the Croft plantation to the Land Commission. Slider informed Scott, "This land must be purchased [by the Land Commission] as a good many of the colored people have already settled upon it and are in a great stew. . . ." If the political maneuver of the Democrats to purchase for themselves the Croft plantation were not thwarted, the Republican party in Newberry would suffer a serious setback. "It would be a great stumbling block in the next election and give the other party something to work on. . . ."[43] The political pressure

41. Judson Lawton to Robert Scott, January 24, 1871, Governor Scott's Papers. See also: Hector Robinson to Governor R. K. Scott, November 26, 1869; G. Whipple to R. K. Scott, January 10, 1871; Ibid.

42. Powel to Scott, November 30, 1868, General Letters File, Governor Scott.

43. Thomas Slider to Governor Robert Scott, February 18, 1870, Governor Scott's Papers.

brought to bear on the Advisory Board resulted in a sacrifice
of the meritorious aspects of the experiment in favor of expediency. The Croft plantation in Newberry was purchased
by the Land Commission at an exorbitant price to protect
the Republican party's interests in that county.[44] The Republicans held Newberry County in the fall election, but the
burden of inflated prices on the Croft lots was passed to the
supposed "beneficiaries" of the Land Commission Act—the
Negroes.

Robert J. Donaldson, Chesterfield's state senator and an
agent for the Land Commission, viewed the experiment as an
instrument for the protection of the up-country Negroes. Since
the freedmen in the up-country counties did not constitute
the majority of the population, Donaldson urged that large
tracts be purchased so that "colonies" of sufficient Negro Republican strength could be established. These "colonies"
would draw the Union people of the up-country and attract
Negro settlers from North Carolina to points where they
would be a power the Democrats could not attack, and would
offer each other mutual support. Specifically, Donaldson considered the Wadsworth property owned by Henry J. Fox as
suitable for the establishment of one such "colony," and he
assured Leslie that the tract could be settled immediately by
thrifty, hard-working Negroes.[45] Five plantations including
the Wadsworth tract were purchased from Fox upon Donaldson's recommendation,[46] and Donaldson, being a partner of
Fox, shared in the proceeds of the sales.[47]

Although Republicans throughout the state presented argu-

44. Purchase Book, Land Commissioner's Office, May 31, 1870, p. 115, S.C.A.
45. R. J. Donaldson to R. K. Scott, September 11, 1869, Governor Scott's
Papers; R. J. Donaldson to C. P. Leslie, October 15, 1869, Samuel Dibble
Papers, Duke University.
46. Advisory Board Minutes, October 21, 1869.
47. Repts. and Resols., 1875–1876, pp. 1246–47.

ments political as well as economic in favor of the speedy settlement of the Negroes upon the Land Commission tracts before the 1870 election, organizational difficulties plagued the commission from its inception. In addition to the lack of trained, responsible administrators, there was substantially no administrative doctrine to guide them. All policies were irregularly and informally conceived. This absence of order affected all areas of state government, and disorganization in the Land Commission simply typified the general lack of formal arrangements in government. For example, although rules were adopted requiring a majority to constitute a quorum, Advisory Board meetings were called at a moment's notice, administrators had to be tracked down, and often the meetings were postponed when a quorum could not be obtained.[48] As simple a remedy as a memorandum, or more formally, regularly scheduled meetings, could have halted this haphazard procedure. Nevertheless, seven months passed before the Advisory Board settled down to regularly scheduled meetings.

Furthermore, the lack of a system for inspecting land offered for sale hampered the experiment and led to large-scale fraud. Land was purchased not only through individual application, but also at sheriffs' sales. Sub-land-commissioners were appointed for most of the 31 counties to seek out good property at public auction. Moreover, since it was inconceivable that the central board sitting in Columbia could appraise each and every tract offered for sale, ostensibly these county agents had been appointed to provide local counsel. It was their responsibility to advise the board on the applications submitted from their locality, selecting those that were acceptable for the purposes set forth in the Land Commission Act. If properly chosen, the deputy commissioners could have furnished the Advisory Board with an effective inspection

48. Advisory Board Minutes, October 6, 1869.

system. Most of Leslie's appointments, however, were based solely on patronage. Records are scarce, but from the fragmentary returns of 13 county agents, it appears that 10 were Republican members of the state legislature and seven of the 10 were Negroes.[49] Since the whole country was attuned to patronage on the county as well as state and national levels, no one seriously questioned Leslie's appointments of agents totally unfamiliar with the quality of land offered for sale in their counties. In some instances the sub-commissioners did serve the board well. For example, Marion County's Negro senator, Henry Hayne, submitted for the board's consideration the Mace tract, consisting of 1,371 acres, including 200 acres of good swamp land, an excellent range for cattle, corn, and grain, and the balance good upland and woodland, which was offered to the state for $1,500.[50] Since Negroes settled on all the lots of the Mace tract as soon as the land had been subdivided, Hayne's recommendation proved well-founded. Nevertheless, most agents' reports were not only less reliable but were actually misleading.

Major Sam Adams, who had served under Scott during the war, seemed a reliable agent to investigate the Burroughs tract in Kershaw County. Adams, in his evaluation of the tract, seems to have relied heavily upon the opinion of the freedmen as to the land's value. Adams quoted the Negroes as agreeing, "There was no better land, and that it was worth a man's money to buy it." Adams supported this opinion stating that if he had the means to invest, he "would not hesi-

49. The 10 Republican sub-land-commissioners were: R. H. Cain, Charleston; Lucius Wimbush, Chester; R. J. Donaldson, Chesterfield; John Lunney, Darlington; Beverly Nash, Edgefield; J. H. Rainey, Georgetown; Henry Cardozo, Kershaw; Henry Hayne, Marion; H. J. Maxwell, Marlboro; and S. A. Swails, Williamsburgh. Donaldson, Lunney, and Maxwell were white. *Repts. and Resols., 1871–1872*, pp. 363–82.

50. Henry Hayne to C. P. Leslie, October 11, 1869, Samuel Dibble Papers.

tate to take the place at twenty-five or twenty-six thousand dollars on speculation. . . ."[51] Never doubting the trustworthiness of Adams, the board leaped to the bait and purchased the Burroughs tract for $22,500.[52] Soon after, they discovered that the market value of the tract had been fixed at $8,000, and that the notorious "scalawag," Franklin Moses, Jr., had manipulated the transaction in his own favor. Aware of the state's interest in the Burroughs tract, Moses had purchased the land at a reduced price from the original owner, and then employed Adams to act as his agent in deceiving the board as to the land's actual worth. Outraged at being duped by Moses and Adams, the board exerted pressure upon Moses to reduce his price. After much give and take the sum of $14,000 was agreed upon.[53]

In the meantime, the Advisory Board sought to eliminate their total dependency upon the questionable agents' reports through a method scarcely more reliable. Approval of purchase in a particular county was to be determined by the recommendation of the board member who resided in that same section of the state. (For instance, all the lands in York County were purchased upon the recommendation of Neagle, a resident of York). Since all the board members except Cardozo were outsiders, unfamiliar with the land they claimed to represent, they could be misled by others, or mislead others, as the case might be. Lands purchased in counties where no member resided usually were appraised not by the sub-land-agent, but by that county's "reputable" men.[54] The "repu-

51. Major S. R. Adams to C. P. Leslie, September 23, 1869, Land Transfer File, 1866–1877. Adams acted as agent for the Land Commission, since Kershaw County did not have its own sub-land-commissioner in 1869.

52. *Repts. and Resols., 1875–1876*, pp. 1175, 1184, 1185.

53. *Ibid.; Repts. and Resols., 1871–1872*, pp. 342–43; Purchase Book, Land Commissioner's Office, June 23, 1870, p. 89.

54. J. L. Neagle to C. P. Leslie, November 17, 1869, Samuel Dibble Papers; *Repts. and Resols., 1871–1872*, pp. 1021–22.

table" men picked to counsel the Advisory Board were for the most part partisan choices, usually Republicans of short residence in the county.

Nor was that all. In May, 1869, five months before the first flurry of purchases, the land commissioner had sought the approval of the board for the appointment as surveyor of Benjamin F. Jackson, a loyal Republican and his personal friend.[55] Jackson was appointed, but only to become another victim of administrative mismanagement. To facilitate his work of surveying and subdividing Land Commission tracts, the plats or deeds should have been made available to him immediately upon purchase. Although the Advisory Board had by January, 1870, spent more than the original $200,000 appropriated by the legislature to buy land, no regular procedure had been adopted for informing the surveyor. Often months passed before the Office of the Secretary of State informed Jackson of lands purchased. Furthermore, Jackson complained that not a single plat given to him was found accurate when tested by resurvey; moreover, he experienced great difficulty in locating boundary lines because many plats had not been checked within 50, and some not within 100 years.[56] Under these circumstances, settlement was delayed.

Indubitably, the inherent weaknesses in the organization of the Land Commission threatened its continued existence. It was imperative that an administrative doctrine be formulated. As early as September, 1869, Leslie balked at what he considered the board's hampering his authority as an independent officer of the commission. He suggested that they allow him

55. Two enclosures: (1) Letter from B. F. Jackson to C. P. Leslie, May 4, 1869; (2) Letter from C. P. Leslie to Advisory Board, May 8, 1869, Land Transfer File, 1866–1877.

56. Report of Benjamin F. Jackson to the Advisory Board, April 28, 1870, Land Transfer File, 1866–1877, Reports 1870.

"to execute and carry out the provisions of the body of the law. . . ." However, if this were contrary to their desires, the board should make its wishes known to him. "I cannot fail to see the imperative necessity of the Advisory Board at once agreeing upon a policy to be pursued and adhered to. . . ." He vowed that any clearcut policy "will be strictly carried out by the Land Commissioner."[57] Dissension, once begun, spread rapidly over the formulation of policy. In October, 1869, Scott tendered his resignation as chairman of the Advisory Board, stating, "Other duties are sufficiently numerous and onerous to justify me in relieving myself of all responsibilities not directly connected therewith."[58] Later, however, under oath before the Joint Special Investigating Committee of Charles P. Leslie, Scott testified that he declined to act for a time with the board because "I had myself been accustomed to the purchase and sales of lands for years and knew that no man could buy lands with any hope of having property that would be desirable without giving it some personal attention. . . ."[59] Scott had insisted that before purchasing property, the land commissioner should have inspected personally each tract of land instead of depending upon the representations of others. When Leslie refused to comply with this demand and the board sustained him, Scott, stung by their rebuke, resigned.

Further criticism was heaped upon Leslie by the secretary of state, Francis L. Cardozo, who presented charges of corruption against the land commissioner and demanded his removal upon their being proven. Again Leslie was upheld by

57. Letter from C. P. Leslie to Advisory Board, September 5, 1869, Land Transfer File.
58. Advisory Board Minutes, October 28, 1869.
59. Legislative System File, Journal of the House, January 9, 1872, p. 19; Repts. and Resols., 1875–1876, pp. 1173–74.

a vote of three to one. The secretary of state chose to follow the governor's course by declining to cooperate any longer with the Advisory Board.[60]

Within two months of Leslie's notice announcing that the Land Commission was ready to transact business, two of the original five members of the Advisory Board had resigned. Within two years the Land Commission was to be publicly labeled "a gigantic folly"—one of the state's most expensive experiments and one that produced greater distress and dissatisfaction than had ever before been legalized or patronized by the State of South Carolina.

60. Advisory Board Minutes, October 27, 28, and 30, 1869.

CHAPTER III

In Search of Personal Aggrandizement

THE HISTORY OF THE LAND COMMISSION during the period 1869–1872 is an example of the moral slump that was characteristic of government at all levels during the Grant era. Although the land experiment was humanitarian in concept, in practice it was sabotaged by internal dissension, riddled with corruption, and harassed by the criticism from the Conservatives. The administrators, although much maligned, seemed no more corrupt or incompetent than other Republican state officials; nevertheless, the "prostrate state" could ill afford the extravagance of greed, dishonesty, and ineptitude.

In search of personal aggrandizement, the land commissioner and members of the Advisory Board participated in a series of fraudulent transactions. In addition to high state officials and county land agents, there were a number of native whites, not hitherto labeled "scalawags," who were encouraged by the low moral tone of the Republican administration to swindle the state. Owners of swamps and malaria-infested regions, or of dry and eroded acres, often entered into corrupt bargains with the land commissioner and the Advisory

Board. Through payment of substantial bribes these worthless acres were purchased as property "suitable" for development by Negro settlers.

To avoid redundancy—since corrupt land practices occurred in all counties and followed the same pattern—only three tracts have been selected to represent the nature of the corruption. The three tracts are the Bates land in Spartanburg County, the Cochran tracts in Oconee and Pickens counties, and the Schley property in Colleton and Charleston counties. Bates and Cochran represent native white South Carolinians, heretofore relatively unknown figures of the period who "cooperated" with the Republican administration, whereas Schley was probably a northern speculator who had come to the South after the war.

Benjamin F. Bates, a large landholder in Spartanburg County, was a descendant of William Bates of Providence, Rhode Island. William Bates, along with other New England master textile mechanics, had come to South Carolina in 1816 to utilize the abundant water power, the ready raw materials, and the cheap labor for the establishment of cotton manufacturing. By 1837 he had built the Rocky Creek factory, later named Batesville.[1] Anthony Bates, William's son, took no part in the management of the Rocky Creek factory, preferring to engage in farming, and became a successful planter in the county. At his death, probably in 1842, he left a large estate in lands and slaves. Anthony Bates had been the father of ten children, one of whom was Benjamin F. Bates,[2] a central figure in the story of Land Commission scandals.

Spartanburg County in the northwestern section of South

1. David Duncan Wallace, *The History of South Carolina* (New York: American Historical Society, 1934), II, pp. 411–12.

2. Spartanburg County Wills, Book D, 1840–1858, (Columbia: W.P.A., 1934), typed copy deposited at S.C.A., pp. 37–39.

Carolina, where Bates was born and raised, presented a marked contrast to the counties of the low country. It was not until after the invention of the cotton gin that any considerable number of men such as William Bates entered the Carolina up-country to establish cotton manufacturing. Until their arrival the Piedmont section had been an area of small land-holdings farmed by independent yeomen. Although after the war of 1812 cotton and slavery invaded the up-country, the immense plantations of rice and cotton worked by masses of slaves remained concentrated in the low country. While the dominant figure in the lower part of South Carolina was the planter, in the up-country it was the sturdy, independent yeoman, growing diversified crops on an individual farm, who remained the central character.

Within the context of the up-country setting, Bates had been a highly respected member of the community—a farmer devoid of planter pretensions, yet possessing thousands of acres of good farm land. Bates was honored by his fellow citizens by being elected to serve in the state legislature from 1852 to 1854.[3] Moreover, during the secession crisis of 1860, he had been chosen one of the vice-presidents of the Minute Men Society. This was a Spartanburg organization patterned after its famous predecessor, whose members were to respond to the first call for military service.[4] As far as can be determined, Bates did not serve in the war, but in its early years was elected to the state legislature. His son, however, B. F. Bates, Jr., was a private in the Arsenal Cadets, Company A.[5]

The explanation for the cooperation of Bates with the Republican regime probably lies in several things, but, appa-

3. J. B. O. Landrum, *History of Spartanburg County* (Atlanta: The Franklin Printing Co., 1900), p. 649.
4. *Ibid.*, pp. 149–50.
5. *Ibid.*, pp. 649, 722.

rently, environment was a more important factor than was
ideology. When the hostilities ended, the up-country section
was comparatively less damaged than the rest of the state by
the actualities of war, death, and the wholesale destruction of
property. Similarly, because the Negroes composed only a
small proportion of the population, that region in relation to
the low country was less affected by the political revolution
induced by the Military Reconstruction Acts. Moreover, a
marked difference of attitude and heritage separated the rural
yeomen of Bates's type and the planters of Charleston, who
had been accustomed to wealth, refinement, and culture. Less
encumbered by the weight of tradition, prestige, and the nos-
talgic symbols of the lost cause, men like Bates apparently
were freer than their counterparts, the Charleston planters, to
act in harmony with the new regime. In addition, the white
Republican minority was largely concentrated in counties
with the smallest Negro population.[6] Bates could therefore
join or not join the Radical party "with less reference either
to the albatross of Negro equality or to other major issues
of Reconstruction policy."[7] Few other whites adjusted as easily
as he to the new order of things. Bates, however, determined
to be on the side of power, joined the Republican party in
1868. Active on the local level in party councils, Bates sought
reward for his services. Considering patronage the logical
order of things, he wrote Scott asking to be appointed census
taker of Spartanburg County,[8] and he received the appointment. But as a Republican officeholder in Spartanburg
County, he had many dangerous moments. He was reviled by
many of his fellow citizens as a traitor to his caste and class.

6. Allen W. Trelease, "Who Were the Scalawags?" *The Journal of Southern
History*, XXIX (November, 1963), 452, 456.

7. *Ibid.*, p. 468.

8. B. F. Bates to Governor Robert K. Scott, March 25, 1869, Legislative
System File, 1866–1877, Census.

The Ku Klux Klan, very active in the up-country, visited his home and threatened his life. Often he was forced to flee to Columbia in the middle of the night to keep out of the reach of angry men.[9] His appointment as census taker must have seemed small remuneration indeed for the many risks involved in being a Republican.

In 1870, suffering financial difficulties, Bates sought relief again from the Party. It was granted, and Bates became the sub-agent for the Land Commission in Spartanburg County. Soon after receiving the appointment he selected his own land as suitable for purchase by the commission, but his application was rejected. In desperation he wrote Governor Scott:

> I had a larg amount of land[,] have been for months trying to affect a Sail to the Land Commissioner. My lands are cheep . . . . DeLarge [the Land Commissioner in 1870] was willing and anx. to buy my land but wrote, have to see the Advisory Bord, Will you be so kind as to aid me in the sail?[10]

Governor Scott responded to his petition by calling a special meeting of the Advisory Board. At the conference De Large presented the application of Bates and spoke in favor of the purchase, whereupon Scott moved that the lands be purchased. Cardozo seconded the motion, which was adopted.[11] Bates was paid $12,620.00 for the 1,976 acres purchased by the state.[12]

On the surface the transaction appeared *bona fide*, with only a slight accommodation on Scott's part on behalf of a party wheelhorse. However, the testimony of Bates before a state legislative investigating committee in 1871 reveals the true nature of how the transactions were conducted. Bates had

9. Letter from E. Cannon to Governor Scott, May 28, 1872, Governor Scott's Papers.
10. B. F. Bates to Scott, September 17, 1870, Governor Scott's Papers.
11. Minutes of the Advisory Board, October 12, 1870.
12. *Ibid.*; Purchase Book, Land Commissioner's Office.

"cooperated" with the second land commissioner, Robert De Large, in defrauding the state. By raising his original asking price of $11,000 to $12,620, Bates defrayed the cost of bribing De Large. Bates testified:

> Some of my friends told me that I would not get my land through unless I paid something. I offered Mr. DeLarge five hundred dollars to close the thing up. He did not accept this. I continued to offer until agreed to leave fifteen hundred dollars in his hands, which was to come out of these checks in payment for the land. The checks were delivered to Mr. DeLarge in my presence for the whole sale. Fifteen hundred dollars were retained by Mr. DeLarge and about ten thousand dollars were given to me by him in checks. . . .[13]

Although in this particular transaction the stakes were low, the excess price being only $1,500 to be divided among De Large and his middlemen, the practice of setting a price higher than the owner originally was willing to take was so commonplace that in its sum total the practice was invitingly lucrative.[14] General M. C. Butler, while being examined by the National Congressional Joint Committee investigating the Ku Klux Klan in South Carolina, admitted that the landowners who submitted to this practice were in many cases native white South Carolinians. Asked if they had not at least lent support to the perpetration of fraud in such cases, he replied: "I confess the owner is to be blamed. . . . It was one universal system of plunder. I never have seen anything like it."[15] He did not think a strictly honest man would do it.

Benjamin Bates, however, was not a strictly honest man.

13. Bates's test., *Repts. and Resols., 1871–1872*, p. 1007.
14. Report of the Joint Special Financial Investigating Committee of the General Assembly, *Repts. and Resols., 1871–1872*, p. 20.
15. Butler's test., *Ku Klux Conspiracy, South Carolina: Testimony Taken by the Joint Select Committee to Inquire into the Conditions of Affairs in the Late Insurrectionary States.* (Washington: 1872), IV, p. 1192–94, cited hereafter as *Ku Klux Conspiracy, S.C.*

Later inquiry into the tracts purchased from Bates by the Land Commission revealed him in a somewhat less passive role, not merely lending support to the perpetration of fraud, but also originating it by misrepresenting the quality of his land. Joel Foster, resident of Spartanburg and Democratic state senator from 1868 to 1872, was also called to testify before the Congressional Joint Committee investigating the Ku Klux Conspiracy. In relation to the Bates transaction, he testified: "I know the general character of some of these lands down here. I have been born and raised not far from there . . . they have been generally considered pretty poor lands, some seemed very poor, and a good many of them have been cut down and worn. . . ."[16]

Foster presented to the committee a letter from J. F. Sloan, the surveyor sent by him to report on the Bates land. Sloan stated that on one tract of 331 acres, the land was very poor, "mostly old fields and gullies, and would not bring $2. per acre from any man or woman that ever had that much money." On another Bates tract of 350 acres Sloan reported, "the government was gouged in the number of acres, though it makes but little difference anyway, for it is one of the poorest places in creation, and not a single acre is under fence." On the 508 acre parcel, he reported, "not 20 acres of original woods [are] on it, but plenty of old barren fields and gullies, and really is not worth one-third the money he got for it. . . ."[17] Thus it appears that, while Land Commissioner De Large had defrauded the board, Bates had pulled off an even bigger swindle, deceiving both De Large and the Advisory Board. With the disclosure of his double dealing, Bates lost the confidence of the party regulars. Nevertheless, he somehow remained afloat, practicing his duplicity well into the Redemption era.

16. *Ibid.*, Foster's test., p. 813.
17. *Ibid.*, pp. 814–15.

In the political campaign of 1872, the Republicans split into two factions—regulars and reformers. This rift within the state party machine coincided with the split within the national Republican party. Bates, having been cast adrift by the regulars, joined the Bolters. Although the Bolters carried eight up-country counties, including Spartanburg, they lost the state to the regular Republican candidate, Franklin Moses, Jr.[18] Unabashed by his recent opposition to the candidacy of Moses, Bates sought appointment as trial justice by the new governor.[19] He went away empty-handed, learning that patronage can be wielded as punishment as well as reward. Restored to some favor after the election of 1874, in which he campaigned vigorously for Chamberlain, Bates's Reconstruction career ended as it had begun with his appointment as census taker.[20]

The transgressions of the native-born Benjamin Bates seem minute in comparison with those of Scott and Cochran. Robert K. Scott, as governor of South Carolina and chairman of the Advisory Board, proved to be one of the worst corrupters of the Land Commission Act. Every Land Commission deed in the up-country counties of Oconee and Pickens established the governor's involvement in land speculation at the expense of the state. He did not act alone. John R. Cochran, of Anderson, was his accomplice in the perpetration of these frauds. In the fall of 1869, M. McLaughlin, a friend of Scott and Cochran's, wrote Scott that the "good Irishman" Cochran desired to sell a tract of land in Anderson County to the commission.

18. Simkins and Woody, p. 468.
19. Letter from M. P. F. Camp to Franklin J. Moses, Jr., April 18, 1873, Governor Moses's Papers, S.C.A.
20. Letter from C. B. Hammett to Daniel H. Chamberlain, December 14, 1874; Bates to Chamberlain, March 25, 1875, Legislative System File, 1866–1877; Chamberlain Appointments 1875, S.C.A.

"I think you would do well to advise the land commissioner to purchase it as it would be a great acquisition to us, . . . as he is of the right stamp, and makes himself felt wherever he may be placed. . . ."[21] Sometime in the interval between October, 1869, and May, 1870, the two men met and made an arrangement beneficial to both. At the Advisory Board meeting of May 6, 1870, Governor Scott moved that five dollars per acre be offered for Cochran's land in Anderson County. The motion was seconded and adopted. At this same meeting five tracts of land in Pickens County and six in Oconee County, also belonging to John Cochran, were considered. In each and every instance it was Governor Scott who moved that the Cochran tract be purchased. All motions were seconded and adopted by the board.[22]

The sanctimonious governor, who had refused to cooperate with the board from November 1, 1869, to March 1, 1870, because of irregularities in Leslie's administration, had returned to his position and through his actions had committed the state to purchasing 4,157 acres of land, ostensibly from Cochran, for the sum of $20,261.50.[23] Sufficient evidence exists to implicate Scott beyond any doubt. Cochran's deeds transferred to the South Carolina Land Commission showed that Scott was part-owner of the tracts he sponsored. In December, 1869, William S. Keese and Newton McCulley had conveyed 11 deeds for land in Oconee and Pickens counties to J. R. Cochran, James W. Harrison, and Robert K. Scott. In order to obscure the governor's involvement in the transaction, Scott and Harrison conveyed to Cochran their undivided two-

21. M. McLaughlin to Robert Scott, October 17, 1869, Governor Scott's Papers.
22. Minutes of the Advisory Board, May 6, 1870.
23. Purchase Book, Land Commissioner's Office.

thirds share by deeds bearing the date May 1, 1870.[24] Thus on
May 6, when Scott recommended Cochran's land for purchase,
Cochran appeared as the sole owner of the land. These doings
somehow got out and caught the attention of the press. The
Columbia correspondent of the Charleston *News* reported the
rumor of the governor's duplicity:

> The purchases were completed on May 20, 1870 and about
> that same date three drafts were drawn in favor of John
> Cochran—three drafts of nearly equal size. Why were these
> drafts so nearly equal? They are said to be $7,000., $7,000.,
> and $6,262. . . . Now we have all heard—and these gentlemen
> do not deny . . .—that a large portion of these lands, if not
> all, were sold to Mr. Cochran by Governor Scott and General
> Harrison.[25]

Moreover, the newspaper carried the account of a rumor
that Scott had first offered his portion of the land directly
to the commission but that Neagle had opposed it, whereupon
the governor concluded his deal with Cochran.[26] Scott denied
the report, claiming to be the friend of the Negro. No one
thought to ask him why, if this were so, he had recommended
for purchase land in the up-country near the mountains,
where there were so few Negroes to settle upon the tracts. In
1872, J. E. Green, the sergeant at arms of the Senate, having
been sent to investigate each state-owned tract, reported that
the Scott-Cochran-Harrison tracts contained exceedingly poor
land, most of it timberless. Unwilling to pay the exorbitant
price the state had paid, few Negroes settled upon the tracts.[27]

24. J. W. Stribling to B. F. Whittemore, May 12, 1871, Land Transfer File,
1866–1877; Record of Sales of Lands to the Land Commission, pp. 119, 121,
123, 125, 129, 135, 137, 139, 141, 143, and 145, S.C.A. This book contains deeds
for lands sold to the Land Commission in 1869 and 1870.

25. August 14, 1870, quoted in Fairfield *Herald*, August 24, 1870.

26. *Ibid.*

27. Annual Report of the Secretary of State to the General Assembly, *Repts.
and Resols., 1872–1873*, pp. 150–51.

Scott's corrupt transactions with the Land Commission were to form part of the grounds for the attempt to impeach him in 1871. Not surprisingly, the Republican-controlled legislature voted down the impeachment resolution. In 1876 another Republican probe of the commission was to bring forth more evidence that implicated Scott in Land Commission frauds.[28] Although proof of Scott's involvement in land speculations at the state's expense also was available to the Redeemers, he was never brought to trial. The former governor returned to Napoleon, Ohio, and became a real estate agent—a most fitting occupation for such an experienced operator. This time the evidence apparently had been suppressed by the chairman of the Joint Investigating Committee who in 1877 was none other than Scott's former partner, John R. Cochran.[29]

The Advisory Board's authorization to purchase Dr. Phillip Schley's land in Charleston and Colleton counties was probably the most flagrant betrayal of trust in the Land Commission's checkered history. Schley's property in Colleton County had been described as better for fishing than farming, while much of the acreage in Charleston County was deemed interminable swamps, utterly worthless.[30] The Schley transactions represent a good deal more than simply another example of the corruption of the law.

Land purchases had proceeded at a breath-taking rate, accompanied by bribe upon bribe and fraud upon fraud. When the Advisory Board momentarily halted to take stock of its

28. Testimony taken before the House Special Committee, *Repts. and Resols., 1875–1876*, pp. 1166–1266, *passim.*
29. *Senate Journal, 1877–1878*, p. 10.
30. Annual Report of the Secretary of State to the General Assembly, *Repts. and Resols., 1872–1873*, pp. 144–45; Butler's test., *Ku Klux Conspiracy*, S. C., IV, pp. 1192–1194; F. L. Cardozo's test., Report of the Special Joint Investigating Committee, *Repts. and Resols., 1871–1872*, p. 1005.

financial situation, $450,000 had already been spent—$250,000 more than the face value of the $200,000 in bonds appropriated by the legislature. The Advisory Board, fearing that a probe would uncover their corruption, turned to the legislature for an additional appropriation to cover their deficiencies.

Late in 1869, Scott, in his capacity as governor, addressed a message to the legislature recommending such an appropriation. He dangled before the representatives' eyes visions of enhancing the credit of the state through the subdivision of large bodies of land, much of it uncultivated, into small productive farms, thereby trebling their value at once, and affording to the same extent an increased basis of taxation as well as more homesteads for the Negroes.[31] Nevertheless, his efforts at persuasion failed. The legislature refused to grant the agency an additional appropriation. The desperate men next approached the legislators separately and informally, asking each one's support for an increase. The leading Negro members of the legislature—Rainey, Whipper, Elliott, Ransier, Nash, and De Large—saw an opportunity to enhance their own position at the expense of the commission. They demanded as the price for their cooperation the removal of Leslie as land commissioner and the appointment of a Negro in his place.[32]

Parker, Neagle, Chamberlain, and Scott, faced with probable ruin if they did not agree to the demands of the powerful

31. Annual Message of Governor Robert K. Scott to the General Assembly, November 24, 1869, Executive Messages Orr & Scott, pp. 166–67, S.C.A.; Anderson *Intelligencer*, December 2, 1869.
32. MS Affidavit signed by Niles G. Parker, January 23, 1878, Samuel Dibble Papers, Duke University; MS Affidavit signed by Franklin J. Moses, Jr., July 28, 1877, MS Affidavit signed by C. C. Bowen, August 10, 1877, Land Transfer File, 1866–1877; Affidavits 1877, S.C.A. There is no reason to doubt the validity of this evidence gathered by the Redeemers. Most of the information contained in the affidavits and cited in this chapter had already been gain-said from testimony presented before the Republican state legislative investigating committee in 1875–1876 (See *Repts. and Resols., 1875–1876*, pp. 1166–1266, *passim*).

Negro clique, attempted to force Leslie out of office in return for the granting of an additional appropriation.[33] Scott called a secret meeting of the Advisory Board to discuss possible methods whereby Leslie could be ousted. He was in favor of removing the land commissioner directly by vote of the board, but the other members, fearing that this underhanded procedure might make Leslie angry enough to seek revenge by exposing them all, refused to act on Scott's suggestion. Parker, Chamberlain, and Neagle recommended informing Leslie of the Negroes' demand and making the best possible terms to secure his resignation.[34] In accordance with this plan, Parker met Leslie in the courtyard of the State House and asked for the land commissioner's resignation. Leslie, knowing how desperate his colleagues were to obtain his resignation, refused to relinquish his office, whereupon Parker, expecting this, asked Leslie how much money it would take to get him out of the way. Leslie replied, "*that* sounds like business. I understand *that* and will give you an answer tomorrow."[35]

Leslie drove a hard bargain. The following day at Parker's home, with Parker, Chamberlain, Neagle, and Franklin J. Moses present, Leslie agreed to resign for $25,000 in cash. To raise this sum, the board devised a scheme to purchase a quantity of land in Charleston County at a small sum per acre. The $25,000 would be made up from the difference in the price actually paid for the land and the price at which it would be charged to the state. Chamberlain agreed to be responsible for seeing that the land commissioner received the sum agreed upon.[36] The conference ended amicably, and the swindlers agreed to complete the matter as quickly as possible.

33. *Ibid.*
34. MS Parker's Affidavit, January 23, 1878.
35. MS C. C. Bowen's Affidavit, August 10, 1877.
36. MS Moses's Affidavit, July 28, 1877; MS Parker's Affidavit, January 23, 1878.

At this stage in the negotiations Leslie, coveting more, increased his demands. Unless they purchased his share in the Greenville and Columbia Railroad co-partnership for $20,000, in addition to the $25,000 already agreed upon, the deal was off. Another meeting was hastily called, this time at Chamberlain's home, to discuss Leslie's new ultimatum. Present were Chamberlain, Leslie, Neagle, Parker, C. C. Bowen, and the New York financial agent, H. H. Kimpton. An agreement was reached whereby Leslie would receive $45,000. In return for the stipulated sum, and to prevent further exactions by the land commissioner, Leslie was ordered to write his letter of resignation that very night, leaving it with Chamberlain until the money was paid to him.[37] In addition, Leslie signed blank land purchase forms to be used by the Advisory Board to purchase the property to pay him off.[38] Since State Treasurer Parker at an earlier conference had mentioned several parcels of land in Charleston and Colleton counties from which money could be made, he was given the responsibility of locating land that could be bought at a price so low that at least $45,000 profit could be realized from the sale.

Parker sent for Z. B. Oakes, a Charleston real estate broker with whom he had transacted considerable business before being elected state treasurer. Parker instructed Oakes: "Sell us the largest quantity of good lands you can in Charleston County and vicinity, and some in Colleton County, for the smallest amount of money, do it quickly, put the prices as low as you can, but not so low that there will be no margin of profit upon it."[39]

There seems to have been no honor even among the thieves.

---

37. Letter of resignation from C. P. Leslie to Advisory Board, February 21, 1870, Secretary of State, Commission Letters, 1870–1878 (loose letter), S.C.A.; MS Bowen's Affidavit, August 10, 1877; MS Parker's Affidavit, January 23, 1878.

38. MS Moses's Affidavit, July 28, 1877.

39. MS Parker's Affidavit, January 23, 1878.

In his commission from Parker, Oakes saw an opportunity to increase his personal fortune by duping the commission in the same manner as the board was deceiving the state. For some time, Louis DeSaussure, another Charleston realtor, had been trying to sell a tract of land belonging to Henry M. Manigault, called "Awendaw." At one time the agent had put the plantation up for auction, but even then no purchaser could be found for the land dubbed "Hell-Hole Swamp." DeSaussure had given up all hope of effecting a sale when Oakes approached him and offered $8,000 for the 12,800 acre plantation. Henry Manigault, formerly one the wealthiest Charleston planters, now living in reduced circumstances, accepted the offer of Oakes. A memorandum of agreement was entered into, dated March 5, 1870, and the deed was made out to Dr. Phillip T. Schley.[40] Schley, the son-in-law of Oakes, apparently was used to cloak in legitimacy his father-in-law's machinations. Similarly, Oakes purchased Wythewood and Ararat plantations near Charleston in the name of P. T. Schley. To the trustee, Dr. William T. Wragg, a member of a prominent pre-Revolutionary South Carolina family, Oakes paid the sum of $10,000.[41] Oakes did not confide to Manigault or to Wragg, the original owners, that he and Schley were acting as agents for the state, or that their lands were earmarked for the establishment of Land Commission settlements.[42] Manigault and Wragg apparently were innocent of the duplicity which their former lands were made to serve.

As soon as these transactions had been concluded, Oakes returned to Columbia with his proposal to sell Awendaw, Wythewood, and Ararat plantations in Charleston County,

40. MS Affidavit signed by Louis D. DeSaussure, November 1, 1877; Memorandum of Agreement, March 5, 1870 (copy), Samuel Dibble Papers.

41. MS Affidavit signed by James Simons, Jr., November 1, 1877, Samuel Dibble Papers.

42. Ibid.; MS DeSaussure's Affidavit, November 1, 1877.

and three additional plantations supposedly owned by Schley in Colleton County—Heyward, Risher, and Martin. Parker, Chamberlain, and Neagle agreed to buy all six. The descriptions of these lands were then inserted on the blank applications left by Leslie and bearing his signature, and these were endorsed by Chamberlain, Parker, and Neagle.[43]

The Manigault plantation purchased at $8,000 was credited to the state at $38,400, while Wythewood and Ararat sold by Wragg for $10,000 were credited to the state at $35,980.[44] Furthermore, Colonel N. Heyward stated that his brother, William Henry Heyward, received $10,000 for the Heyward plantation in Colleton County, which was credited to the state at $24,000.[45] The Risher and Martin plantations were charged to the state at $22,374,[46] although the original owners received only $12,000. Altogether, for the sum of $120,754, the state received six plantations valued at approximately $40,000. Leslie received as his share $45,000, Oakes made a tidy profit on his deft land operation, and the remainder was presumably spread among other "interested" parties. Before the sales were formally concluded Leslie was paid in full. Chamberlain collected the money—$45,000 in three separate checks[47]—from the Carolina National Bank. Thereupon Leslie's resignation was formally accepted on March 1, 1870, and Robert C. De Large, a Negro, was appointed land commissioner.[48]

Nor did matters end there. The board, anxious to complete the transaction so they could pay off Leslie, appoint a new

43. MS Application Phillip Schley to Land Commissioner, February 18, 1870, Samuel Dibble Papers.

44. Purchase Book, Land Commissioner's Office.

45. Col. N. Heyward's test., *Repts. and Resols., 1871–1872*, pp. 1015–16; Purchase Book, Land Commissioner's Office; Col. Nathaniel Heyward to Robert K. Scott, January 15, 1871, Governor Scott's Papers.

46. *Ibid.*

47. MS Moses's Affidavit, July 28, 1877.

48. Minutes of the Advisory Board, March 1, 1870.

land commissioner, and get on with the business of securing an additional appropriation, failed to examine Schley's title to the Colleton property. Although not informed of their past dealings, Cardozo, who had refused to sit with the board from the fall of 1869 until after Leslie's resignation in March, suspected that fraud had been committed in his absence. He offered a resolution to appoint a committee of two members to investigate the Schley purchases.[49] Chamberlain, probably trying a red-herring maneuver, seconded the resolution, which was adopted, and Cardozo and Chamberlain formed the two-man committee. Chamberlain, in his capacity as attorney general, now got around to examining Schley's title to the Colleton property, only to find that much of it had been mortgaged by Schley. Apparently Chamberlain then blamed Parker for putting his trust in Oakes, thereby bungling the affair. At the next meeting the innocent Cardozo reported to the members that on the basis of Chamberlain's findings the transaction was "unjust and illegal." Scott went one step further, and in "righteous" indignation moved that the attorney general be authorized to employ necessary legal assistance against the parties concerned. This was seconded by Cardozo and adopted.[50]

With Cardozo poking about and Chamberlain sustaining him, it appeared that Parker was to be made the scapegoat. He, however, fought back. Chamberlain was warned by Parker's New York lawyer not to reveal his findings, because if he did, "Mr. Cardozo is the only State official who would not be carried down and made odious to every honest man."[51] On the same day, the lawyer wrote Parker urging him to tell Cham-

49. *Ibid.*, April 28, 1870.
50. *Ibid.*, May 24, 1870.
51. D. M. Porter to D. H. Chamberlain, June 6, 1870 (Porter's copy), Samuel Dibble Papers.

berlain that the mortgage had been paid: "Hurry it up. Make Schley do it, not yourself."[52] Chamberlain, evidently frightened by the threat, did not bring the case to a jury. Although Parker pressured Schley to pay off the mortgages, titles to the lands were not recorded until November 28, 1871—almost two years after payment had been made.[53]

Although the title to "Hell-Hole Swamp" in Charleston County was clear, the swamp was valueless for settlement unless drained. E. W. Seibels, an Edgefield Democrat, and secretary and treasurer during the Union Reform party canvass of 1870, claimed that the Manigault plantation was full of snakes and alligators and the tract could not be cut up and sold to settlers. Furthermore, when Van Trump, the Democratic member of the Ku Klux Klan investigating committee, asked General M. C. Butler if he knew personally the character of "Hell-Hole Swamp," the planter replied, "an alligator can hardly live there—an alligator could, I suppose, but a human being could hardly."[54] A less partisan description of the property was given by J. E. Green, who was sent by Cardozo in 1872 to investigate all Land Commission tracts. He reported that a preliminary survey of "Hell-Hole Swamp" had been made, and 1,000 acres had been divided into lots for settlement. "About 2,000 acres more [of the 12,800 acres] is capable of cultivation; the balance is an interminable swamp, and utterly worthless."[55] The subdivision of "Hell-Hole Swamp" never was completed, the task proving too difficult. In 1878, Parker attempted to justify the state's purchase of it, claiming the property to be well-timbered and very valuable if drained.[56] Parker's excuse, needless to say, totally ignored the purpose of

52. D. M. Porter to N. G. Parker, June 6, 1870, Samuel Dibble Papers.
53. Purchase Book, Land Commissioner's Office.
54. Seibels' test., *Ku Klux Conspiracy, S.C.,* III, p. 110; Butler's test., IV, p. 1192.
55. *Repts. and Resols., 1872–1873,* p. 144.
56. MS Parker's Affidavit, January 23, 1878.

the Land Commission. The property, even if it were valuable if drained, was worthless for providing small homesteads; heavy capital investment and a combination of proprietors would have been needed to restore this former rice plantation to anything like its original value. This was hardly an undertaking for the poor.

The Advisory Board, as perpetrators of the great land fraud, felt that the end justified the means. To achieve its immediate goal the board showed no concern for the future, allowing the expense of its fiscal irresponsibility to be borne by the Negroes who would have to purchase the land at inflated prices. On the same day, March 1, 1870, that payment was made to the Negro legislators by means of De Large's appointment as land commissioner, the South Carolina legislature amended the Land Commission Act of 1869, appropriating an additional sum of $500,000.[57]

Both actions—the appropriation and the appointment of De Large—were regrettable. In appropriating $500,000, most of which went to cover the Advisory Board's past spending, the legislature made itself an accomplice of the Advisory Board in its corruption and in its betrayal of the land experiment. De Large was an unfortunate choice, since he had no more faith in the people of his race than the former commissioner, Leslie, nor was he any more of a friend to the Negro than his white predecessor had been. In a letter to Governor Scott, De Large revealed the contempt he felt toward his supporters. "I plays them as a fisherman does a fish, I never consents but I don't say no, I will play to employ on the street our friends, and control or divide that influence."[58] Soon after his appointment, De Large was involved in the Bates transaction along with many others, though by the time he assumed office the majority of the money transactions had already occurred.

57. *Statutes at Large*, XIV, pp. 385–86.
58. De Large to Scott, July 13, 1869, Governor Scott's Papers, S.C.A.

CHAPTER IV

"The Gigantic Folly"

OPPOSITION TO THE RADICAL Republican government made its appearance in the spring of 1870 when a convention of Conservative (Democratic) and anti-Radical newspaper men assembled in Columbia to discuss means by which the state could rid itself of corrupt Republican rule. The result of these deliberations was the calling of a state convention to be held on June 15, and out of which emerged the Union Reform party.

The men who assembled at the June convention were realists. Every effort had to be made to conciliate the Negro and to attract him to their banner, because according to the census of 1870 there were 62,547 qualified white voters and 85,475 Negro voters in South Carolina.[1] The new party was to be nonpartisan; the platform adopted declared the 15th Amendment was to be obeyed as fundamental law and that the political and social changes brought about by the war should be considered principles "having the force and obligation of law."[2]

---

1. U. S. Census, 1870, I, 619; cited in Simkins and Woody, p. 450.
2. Platform of the Union Reform Party and The Address of the Executive Committee to the People of the State, *Pamphlets, Reconstruction in South Carolina, Democratic and Republican, 1869–1880* (bound copy), S.C.L.; Charleston *News*, June 17, 1870.

The party nominated for governor Richard B. Carpenter, a Republican lawyer from Kentucky. A resident of South Carolina since 1867, Carpenter had been appointed judge of the First Circuit, holding that office from 1868 to July, 1870. Selected as his running mate was General Matthew C. Butler, a highly esteemed Democrat and a native of Edgefield County.[3] The delegates considered their selection of candidates a real challenge to the Republicans. It was hoped that Carpenter would attract both Negro and white Republican voters, while his teammate, Butler, would draw upon his popularity with the Democratic minority.[4]

Since strength is found in unity, the first aim of the Union Reform party was to strike a balance among the diverse elements composing its organization. The majority within the party, although not free of racial prejudice, recognized the need to accommodate themselves to the new political order—a Negro majority. But a smaller group, by no means impotent, was unreconciled to the idea of Negro participation in government. These men were determined to restore the pre-war ruling oligarchy and to subordinate the freedmen to their former masters. They addressed themselves directly and continuously to the passions and prejudices of the suppressed white minority. A third group, differing only slightly from the majority, disputed the right of those who paid little or no taxes to levy taxes for the state. According to this group, later to give voice to their opposition at the Taxpayers' Convention in 1871, the frauds in the Land Commission alone had increased the taxpayers' burden by over $600,000 in a single year. This sum "before the war, would have paid the expenses of the State, for one year and a half . . . ."[5]

3. *Ibid.*; Simkins and Woody, pp. 447–49; *Ku Klux Conspiracy, S.C.*, III, Seibels' test., p. 95, Suber's test., p. 152, Carpenter's test., p. 235.

4. *Ibid.*

5. *Proceedings of the Taxpayers' Convention of 1871* (Charleston: Edward Perry, Printer, 1871), p. 22.

Since reform in government was the only platform on which all the opposition could stand united, the Union Reform party entered the campaign pleading for deliverance from a corrupt Republican administration. The strategy of the opposition was to find an issue that could strike a note of response with the Negro voters and cause them to desert their Republican allies. The revelations of blatant corruption within the administration of the Land Commission was one such issue that might attract many Negro adherents. Jonas Byrd, a Negro delegate to the reform convention, expressed feelings of disillusionment, shared by many of his race, with the Reconstruction government. Byrd, a long-time resident of Charleston, although proudly proclaiming his Republican affiliation, told the convention he refused "to continue a set of men in office who, while their right hand grabs yours in sembled friendship, their left hand is stealing its way to your purse." He cited the Advisory Board as a body of dishonest administrators who, "while . . . they have pretended to give homes to the homeless and land to the landless, scarce a poor man has a piece of land; while in one transaction . . . the Land Commission defrauded, nay, stole from the State $90,000."[6]

The editor of the *Missionary Record*, the most influential Negro newspaper in the state, had made known to his readers his distress over the radical departure of the land experiment from its original concept. Editor Richard Cain, the proponent of Negro landownership at the convention of 1868, vehemently attacked the late land commissioner Leslie.

> The act creating the commission we regard as a success, and would have proved such had the mantle of responsibility fallen upon the shoulders of an honest well wisher of the poor. But unfortunately for the cause of suffering humanity,

---

6. Columbia *Guardian*; cited in Anderson *Intelligencer*, June 23, 1870.

it fell where the springs had dried up, where there was no sympathy nor interest, save that of peculation. Two hundred thousand dollars of bonds were issued under the direction of the Commission, which had all been expended before the meeting of the last Legislature, and only forty-five thousand acres of land bought according to the statement of the commissioner. Last session resolutions were offered in the General Assembly requesting him to report the condition of his office, and what had been done, yet at no time could a report be elicited. Subsequently a change was made in that office, but unlike any other officer of government, Mr. Leslie has not yet turned over his books and papers to his successor. No report has been submitted to the Governor or advisory board. No one seems strong enough to bring Mr. Leslie to account for his disregard of a plain duty as a state officer.[7]

As criticism against Leslie and the Advisory Board mounted, Governor Scott became frightened. Fearing a reform impulse might overwhelm him in the fall election, he consulted a Columbia lawyer, Colonel J. D. Pope, to determine whether or not Leslie's "alleged" fraudulent transactions could be brought under review in the courts.[8] If so, Scott probably intended to make Leslie the scapegoat, the sole administrator responsible for the corrupt practices that had denied Negroes the fruits of owning property. That way Scott could have assumed the pose of a reformer, stealing the opposition's thunder by instituting reform within the ranks of the Republican party. According to Scott, Pope informed him that although great irregularities had undoubtedly been practiced to the injury of the state, he did not possess the necessary legal proofs. Legal evidence could only be furnished by those who sold the lands, and by those effecting such sales and profiting

7. *Missionary Record*, May 1, 1870; cited in Anderson *Intelligencer*, May 5, 1870.
8. Robert K. Scott to J. D. Pope, May 4, 1870 (Scott's copy), Loose Papers, Governor Scott's Papers.

by them. Pope stated that since they were unlikely to incriminate themselves, he could not proceed with court action.[9] This apparently satisfied Scott. If Pope could not gain possession of legal proofs, Scott probably reasoned, neither could the opposition substantiate *their* charges against the Land Commission. In any case he dropped the matter.

Leslie, displaying his habitual lack of restraint, sought to exonerate himself by putting all the blame on the Advisory Board. Perhaps he knew of Scott's correspondence with Pope, but probably he was enraged over the Republican administration's failure to come to his defense. In a letter to the Columbia *Daily Guardian*, he issued a general denial, claiming that he had not bought a foot of land in South Carolina while he was land commissioner; never had he had $1.00 of Land Commission money in his hands; neither had the Advisory Board bought one foot of land on his recommendation; nor had he ever drawn an order on the land funds—"I never was Land Commissioner, only in name . . . . I have got sick and tired of forever being assailed."[10]

As the fall election drew near, the Reformers stepped up their campaign. Seibels, the secretary and treasurer of the Union Reform party, C. H. Suber, Democratic lawyer from Newberry, and Colonel John W. Harrington, a planter in Marlboro County, as well as Carpenter and Butler, intensified their attack upon the corruptions of the Land Commission. Butler, while campaigning, charged that the Land Commission was the blackest spot on the Republican administration record. Visiting all thirty-one counties, the Reformers exposed one Land Commission fraud after another, in each place focusing their assault upon whatever scandals had been committed

9. Message of Governor Scott to the General Assembly, January 9, 1872, Legislative System File, 1872.

10. July 24, 1870; cited in Charleston *Tri-Weekly Courier*, July 26, 1870.

in that particular county.[11] In their attacks the speakers avoided making any mention of abolishing the commission, assailing only the evils then in practice. Thus, in Chesterfield County Carpenter disclosed to his audience that Dr. H. J. Fox had bought a tract of land for $10,000 and had subsequently sold it to the Land Commission for $36,000.[12] Colonel Harrington in his speech at Cheraw revealed Senator Donaldson's part in a fraud committed in that county, Marlboro. Donaldson, Harrington told his large Negro audience, had bought 800 acres from a Mr. Gooch for $7,750 but had required a receipt for $10,000. It was the latter amount that the state was made to pay, and Donaldson pocketed $2,250. In addition, though the land was poor (being valued at only $2,000, or less than $3.00 an acre), it had cost the state $12 to $13 per acre, and this is what the Negro would pay for it.[13] In this manner the Reformers hoped to capture the votes of those cheated out of land by an Advisory Board "who are growing fat on the sweat, the industry, and the blindness of the people of our state."[14]

In the meantime the Republicans were not idle; they too entered the campaign with energy, for the Union Reform party was a threat to their continued existence. At their convention they renominated Scott and chose as his running mate for lieutenant governor a Negro from Charleston, Alonzo J. Ransier. They charged that the Reformers were wolves in sheep's clothing, Democrats disguised as non-partisans. In general, they dismissed as false the Reformers' accusations of cor-

11. Butler's test., *Ku Klux Conspiracy, S.C.*, IV, pp. 1192–94, 1214–15; Seibels' test., III, pp. 95, 109–11; Suber's test., p. 152, Carpenter's test., pp. 235, 269–70.
12. *Tri-Weekly Courier*, September 10, 1870.
13. *Ibid.*; Presentment of Grand Jury of Marlboro, September 24, 1870 (copy), "Fraudulent Transaction between R. J. Donaldson and J. H. Gooch," Legislative System File, 1866–1877, S.C.A.
14. *Tri-Weekly Courier*, August 2, 1870.

ruption and dishonesty and insisted that only the presence of the Republican party in South Carolina prevented the complete erosion of the Negro's rights.[15] In addition, the Republicans sought to convince them that the whites wished neither the breakup of the plantations into small farms nor any tampering with their labor supply because the independent black landowner would refuse to work on shares.[16] At the same time, within the Advisory Board, Cardozo, Chamberlain, and Scott urged De Large to get on with the business of surveying the Land Commission tracts so that the Negroes could be sold property before the election,[17] thereby discrediting the opposition's charges of corruption and preventing the land-hungry Negroes from deserting the party.

Throughout the 1870 campaign the Union Reform party was pressed to refute the Republican accusation that it was the party of privilege for whites only. Though the Reformers insisted that their concern was for every citizen, whatever his status and whatever his color, their assertions of nonpartisanship were never wholly convincing. The majority of Negroes rejected the Reformers' appeal, believing that if a party of white men came to power they themselves would lose their political and civil rights.[18] In the election Scott and Ransier polled 85,071 votes while the Union Reform candidates received 51,537; the result closely paralleled the number of Negro and white voters in the state.[19] Failure to win over the

15. Simkins and Woody, pp. 449–50.

16. I. L. B. Gilmore to Governor Robert K. Scott, November 17, 1870, General Letters File, Nov.–Dec. 1870, S.C.A.; Charleston *Daily Republican*, June 2, 1870, cited an editorial in Fairfield *Herald* to substantiate this charge. Desportes, editor of the *Herald*, had written that the opportunity to acquire land cheaply through the Land Commission had produced disastrous results, and he warned his readers, "It will render your Negro hirelings for a while less efficient and more sullen and discontented" (September 8, 1869).

17. Minutes of the Advisory Board, August 2, 1870.

18. Williamson, p. 356.

19. Simkins and Woody, p. 453.

Negro had meant defeat for the Reformers, and not until 1876, by employing different methods and new leaders, did an opposition party triumph. Nevertheless, their cries of corruption had become a trumpet blast, thoroughly frightening the Republican administration. To forestall indignant South Carolinians from rising in open rebellion, reform was begun within the ranks of the dominant party.

Directly after the election of 1870 the Radical-controlled legislature[20] launched a probe of the Land Commission. Leslie had courted an investigation of the commission as early as eight days after his resignation from that office—March 9, 1870 —and on the floor of the Senate the former commissioner, still a senator from Barnwell County, had expostulated: "There is a class of dirty, yelping curs, who are always barking at the Land Commission. But where is the man, on or off this floor, who can lay his hand upon a single act of that Commission and say it is wrong. If you want an investigation ask for it."[21]

Now, after the Reformers had exposed corruption within the commission, Leslie was taken at his word. A fellow Republican, Senator E. S. J. Hayes, of Lexington County, introduced a resolution calling for a special committee of three senators and five representatives to be appointed to investigate transactions of the Land Commission, past and present. The resolution was referred to the Committee on Public Lands, which reported in favor of it. Leslie, himself a member of the Public Lands Committee, endorsed the report.[22] The resolution passed in the Senate, the House concurred, and in due time

20. In 1870, House; 49 white, 75 black; 22 Reformers, 1 Independent, 101 Radicals; Senate: 20 white, 10 black; 24 Radicals, 5 Reformers, 1 Independent.
21. Fairfield *Herald*, March 9, 1870.
22. *Senate Journal, 1870–1871*, pp. 31, 56; Report of the Committee on Public Lands on the Resolution of the Investigation of the Transactions of the Land Commissioner, Majority Report, December 9, 1870, Land Transfer File, 1866–1877, Resolutions Committee Reports, S.C.A.

Senators Hayes, Owens, and Foster and Representatives Braw-
ley, Gardner, Berry, Saunders, and Lee were appointed to
form the Special Joint Investigating Committee.[23]

The Republicans apparently intended to give only lip service to the idea of reform. Once this committee was formed,
its members took little interest in pursuing a real investigation; on many occasions Senator Joel Foster of Spartanburg,
the lone Democratic member of the committee, was the only
one present. Since Hayes, the chairman, was rarely there, Foster was asked by the clerk to take charge of the investigation.
Contrary to Radical expectations, Foster pushed ahead and
examined many witnesses in his search for legal proof of Land
Commission corruption.[24] Moreover, in February, 1871, a
Joint Special Financial Investigating Committee was established by the legislature to investigate all the financial transactions of the state. Under this concurrent resolution a second
committee began its probe of the Land Commission.[25] These
investigations were to drag on throughout the entire year of
1871, but in the meantime the operations of the Land Commission flowed on uninterrupted.

2

Although an additional $500,000 had been appropriated on
March 1, 1870, no lands were purchased by the Advisory Board
for over two months. The inactivity stemmed from Leslie's
refusal to turn over his records to De Large, and the board
suspended operations until the extent of previous expenditures could be determined. At the end of April the treasurer

23. *Senate Journal 1870–1871*, pp. 111, 125, 130.
24. Foster's test., *Ku Klux Conspiracy, S. C.*, IV, pp. 825–26, 832.
25. *Senate Journal, 1870–1871*, pp. 406–07; *House Journal, 1870–1871*, p. 406.

reported that $476,147.94 had been spent, leaving a balance of $223,852.06.[26] The passage of the second appropriation had covered the board's reckless spending.

Although the largest money transactions of the commission had been completed before De Large took office, his administration was also stained by corruption. De Large, a light mulatto, had been a tailor in Charleston before the war. He had emerged in the early post-war years as an organizer of freedmen's meetings, parades, and celebrations. De Large was a shrewd young politician who came to have unlimited influence over the Negroes in Charleston.[27] It was during his tenure as land commissioner that the Bates and Cochran-Scott purchases were consummated. Whereas Leslie refused to turn over his records to the Advisory Board, De Large kept none.[28]

Allegedly, Scott had arranged for De Large's appointment as land commissioner so that the latter could swindle enough money from the commission to finance his campaign for the Congressional seat of Christopher C. Bowen, one of Scott's bitterest political enemies.[29] In the interim, before purchases were resumed, De Large had given his attention to hurrying up the subdivision of Land Commission tracts. By June 1, 1870, according to the surveyor's report, 24 tracts had been subdivided into 654 homesteads.[30] Since these tracts represented only a small portion of the state's holdings, De Large instructed Jackson, the Land Commission's surveyor, to com-

26. Minutes of the Advisory Board, April 28, 1870.

27. Charleston *News*, September 12, 1868; *News and Courier*, February 16, 1874; Simkins and Woody, p. 132; Williamson, p. 369.

28. *Repts. and Resols., 1871–1872*, pp. 333–34.

29. Charleston *Daily Republican*, March 2, 1870; MS Affidavit, signed by N. G. Parker, January 23, 1878, Samuel Dibble Papers.

30. Report of Benjamin F. Jackson, Surveyor L.C.S.C., June 1, 1870, Land Transfer File, 1866–1877.

plete the subdivision of the remaining plantations, especially in the low country, as soon as possible. The matter was vital to De Large's own interest as well as to that of the party. The land commissioner needed a more impressive record to put before the voters in his congressional campaign against Bowen. Jackson assured De Large that before the end of the year "at least 3,000 families containing about 15,000 persons will be settled in homes of their own in the low country."[31] He reported that most of the tracts had been well adapted to division into small farms for settlement by homesteaders, and that "every lot, however small is provided with wood—and whenever possible—with water—."[32] Nevertheless, his judgment as to the quality of the lands he surveyed is questionable. Included in a later report to De Large was the following revealing item: "In some of the more malarious districts, it was impossible to commence the surveys until after frost."[33] It was probably fortunate for De Large that the "malarious districts" were not surveyed until after the election. At any rate, De Large, despite the taint of corruption, successfully used the office of land commisioner as a steppingstone to Congress, and after his election to the United States House of Representatives he resigned from the Land Commission in March, 1871.[34]

Meanwhile Richard Cain had written Scott urging his assistance in securing the post in case De Large should resign: "This land business, is one in which I have a deep interest . . . . I write this early because I am anxious for the position that I may be more useful to my people and to the state in settling

31. Letter of Benjamin F. Jackson to R. C. De Large, November 15, 1870, Drawer 51, Division of General Services, S.C. Record Center, Columbia.

32. Ibid.

33. Report of Benjamin F. Jackson to R. C. De Large, February 23, 1871, Land Transfer File, 1866–1877.

34. Minutes of the Advisory Board, March 1, 1871.

the people in their homes, and encouraging industry, and honesty."[35]

Although Cain at that time was probably the most suitable person for the appointment, possessing intellect, energy, and managerial qualities, his stand in the reform movement of 1870 apparently disqualified him in the eyes of the Republican party. And yet the appointment was not made recklessly. By this time neither the whites nor the blacks would have tolerated another Leslie or De Large. State Senator Henry Hayne, a mulatto from Marion County, won appointment as the third and final land commissioner. During the war he had been a sergeant in the First South Carolina Volunteers and had represented Marion County at the constitutional convention of 1868.[36] Active in Land Commission affairs since the beginning, Hayne had been noted for his honesty as Marion's deputy land commissioner. At this time honesty was a quality so rare that its mere possession distinguished the man and made his appointment acceptable to all.

Since all the funds of the commission had been spent during De Large's tenure, Hayne was instructed by the Advisory Board in March, 1871, to close out all the commission's unfinished business.[37] His assignment was frustrated by De Large's refusal to cooperate. For five months Hayne's predecessor avoided turning over his books and papers. The reason for De Large's procrastination became clear when the keys to the safe were finally turned over to Hayne. The books stacked neatly inside were as blank as they had been the day they came from

35. R. H. Cain to Robert Scott, November 1, 1870, General Letters File, Nov.–Dec., 1870. Ultimately, Cain was indicted for fraud in connection with a land deal; his case, however, was never brought to trial (Charleston *Daily News*, January 14, 1873; *New York Times*, June 15, 1874; Williamson, p. 207.
36. Reynolds and Faunt, p. 235; Williamson, pp. 29, 145.
37. Minutes of the Advisory Board, March 1, 1871.

the stationer's. Since no information could be obtained from De Large's "records," Hayne sent out circular letters to all deputy land commissioners to find out what sums had been paid in by the Negro settlers in the various counties.[38]

Many agents failed to respond. Therefore Hayne decided to inspect personally each tract, confront each of his recalcitrant agents, and demand of them an accurate account of payments received from Land Commission settlers. The Advisory Board, however, refused to appropriate money for his travel expenses, thereby preventing Hayne from discovering the true condition of the land.[39] Receiving very little cooperation from either the Advisory Board or the deputy county commissioners, and with no funds at his disposal, Hayne in his report to the legislature in November, 1871, admitted his inability to carry out all his duties.[40] Although Hayne's report could shed little light on the operations of the Land Commission, the findings of the two legislative investigating committees were being readied at about the same time for presentation to the legislature.

One year had passed since the legislature had taken steps to initiate reforms. Although the reforming impulse was initially more symbolic than actual, Democratic Senator Joel Foster of Spartanburg, in seeking to find evidence of Land Commission corruption, had combined forces with C. P. Leslie, who allegedly was seeking to exonerate himself from the taint of scandal. In July of 1871, Senator Foster had testified before the Congressional Ku Klux Conspiracy Committee that while he had acted as chairman of the Special Joint Investigating Committee of the Land Commission, Leslie had come frequently

38. Report of the Land Commissioner to the General Assembly, *Repts. and Resols., 1871–1872*, pp. 333–34, 361.
39. *Ibid.*, p. 334.
40. *Ibid.*, pp. 333–38.

into the committee room, "hunting up sending for and bringing witnesses . . . . He took the privilege of asking some questions and was very rigid in his examination." Furthermore, as
Foster related to the committee, Leslie had told him: "I want
you to ferret this thing out rigidly, and if you can find anything for or against me, I want it known."[41] Although the
testimony before Foster's committee was still incomplete in
July, 1871, the Spartanburg senator was convinced that the
testimony to that date exonerated Leslie of guilt, and in his
place convicted De Large and the Advisory Board.[42] However,
the report submitted to the General Assembly in November,
1871, was that of the Joint Special Financial Investigating
Committee (the second committee), and it turned out to be an
arraignment of Leslie and an overall censure of the Advisory
Board.[43] The committee denounced the entire Land Commission as a "gigantic folly about which there has been more said
and less known than any other branch of the State Government."[44] It declared:

41. *Ku Klux Conspiracy, S.C.*, IV, p. 823.
42. *Ibid.*, pp. 810–33, *passim*.
43. *Repts. and Resols., 1871–1872*, Appendix, pp. 7–297. The committee
making the report to the General Assembly in November, 1871, was the Joint
Special Financial Investigating Committee appointed by the legislature in
February, 1871. The members of this second committee to investigate the
Land Commission were B. F. Whittemore and S. A. Swails for the Senate;
for the House, John B. Dennis, W. H. Gardner, Jr., and Timothy Hurley.
They had been gathering evidence and questioning witnesses concurrently
with Foster's committee. The latter failed to report, because Foster refused
to sign the record of the testimony taken before him as chairman *pro tempore*.
In a letter to the stenographer he gave as the reasons for his refusal, the in-
completeness of the testimony, and that as it stood "the public might suppose
I was acting in the interest of the former Land Commissioner, Hon. C. P.
Leslie" (Joel Foster to Gil Dixon Fox, December 15, 1871, Committee Reports,
1871, Legislative Papers File, S.C.A.). Apparently Foster had come to believe
he had been duped by Leslie. The quotations cited in this paper are taken
from the report of the second committee; the only publication of Foster is the
testimony of witnesses taken before his committee (*Repts. and Resols., 1871–
1872*, pp. 1005–27).
44. *Repts. and Resols., 1871–1872*, Appendix, p. 14.

A more outrageous and enormous swindle could not have been perpetrated, and a more subtle manner of concealment perfected. By the exhibit it will be seen who had been the recipients of "favors" from this source of extravagance, the amounts paid them, and, as far as possible what for. It will be observed that men in high places through their kinsmen and trusty friends, have not been unmindful of the opportunity to make "an honest penny," nor have they been forgotten in the decisions of the Advisory Board when advising upon purchases to be made. It is a presumption that is almost conclusive, that unless some consideration was presented to some of the Advisory Board worthy of a decision in favor of the purchase of any tract of land, such decision would be withheld, and, however fair the offer, or just the price asked, the applicant would meet with no encouragement . . . .[45]

It appeared, moreover, that of the 168 state-owned tracts, a large portion were "either inaccessible, or so poor that the class of people for whom the public lands were intended, will not be anxious to settle, or able, out of the products of such lands, to pay for them . . . ."[46] The report concluded with the statement that the only satisfaction or comfort that South Carolinians could take was that having expended more than the entire amount authorized by law, "the purposes of the Land Commission *have been gained*, and no further expenditures can be made."[47]

"Outrageous and enormous swindles" had been perpetrated by other financial agencies as well. The committee held indisputable proof, it declared, that the financial offices of the state—the Financial Board, the New York financial agent, Kimpton, the Sinking Fund Commission, and the governor himself—had all disguised the true financial condition of South Carolina.

45. *Ibid.*, p. 20.
46. *Ibid.*, p. 21.
47. *Ibid.*

The question remains as to how Scott avoided impeachment when his part in defrauding the state became known. The Anderson *Intelligencer* reported that in the months of October and November, 1871, Scott invested $100,000 in real estate in his hometown of Napoleon, Ohio. His salary as assistant commissioner of the Freedmen's Bureau for two years paid him $7,000 while his salary as governor for three years equaled $15,000, totaling $22,000. The editor wondered how Scott accumulated the remaining $78,000.[48]

The Joint Special Financial Investigating Committee provided an answer:

> Nor has the Executive himself been behind his peers, if collateral testimony is sufficient, in his eagerness through "confidential friends," "old army buddies," or handy resident relatives, to sell tracts of land to the State, and receive the highest possible price for the same without reference to the real value. His frequent outbursts of indignation over "the damned swindle" as he calls it, are but the cloakings of his confederation with such as have "stolen from the Treasury," by a concert of purpose that made the action sure.[49]

As stated earlier, on the basis of the evidence of the Financial Investigating Committee, an attempt was made by the governor's own party to impeach him. C. C. Bowen, one of Scott's political opponents, then a legislator from Charleston, introduced a resolution on December 18, 1871, to impeach Scott and Parker for high crimes and misdemeanors.[50] Scott now resorted to bribery in order to defeat the resolution on impeachment. According to Hasting Gantt, a Negro legislator from Beaufort, his delegation had assumed that the resolution would not be brought to a vote until after the Christmas re-

48. December 14, 1871.
49. *Repts. and Resols., 1871–1872*, Appendix, p. 20.
50. *New York Times*, December 19, 1871; Simkins and Woody, p. 162.

cess and had decided to return home for the holidays one day before the session was to close. As Gantt was leaving the State House to go to the train station, he was approached by Colonel John J. Patterson, the "carpetbagger" from Pennsylvania. Patterson, who in 1872 was to spend enormous sums to secure his election to the United States Senate, asked Gantt not to go before the impeachment question was settled. Gantt related to Patterson his delegation's belief that the impeachment question would not be voted on until after the recess and assured him that when the matter did come up he would not vote to impeach Scott. Gantt testified that Patterson then offered him a bribe. "If I would wait, and didn't go home until the recess, he would give me two hundred dollars."[51] Gantt refused Patterson's bribe and went home. Others were bribed and stayed.[52] Scott called an extra session of the legislature to meet on December 23, 1871, to vote on the pending resolution.[53] The impeachment proceedings were voted down.[54]

The South Carolina legislature, nevertheless, took steps to atone for the past. On February 15, 1872, the act creating the office of land commissioner was repealed. All books and papers pertaining to that office were turned over to the secretary of state. Henceforth the secretary of state was to execute the duties of the land commissioner.[55]

Labeled a "gigantic folly" because its offenses had been very bad indeed, the South Carolina Land Commission had nevertheless created a base upon which a great number of Negro families might establish themselves as independent

51. "Testimony of Hasting Gantt before the Joint Investigating Committee," Legislative System File, Reports of Committee, 1877, S.C.A.

52. Simkins and Woody, p. 162.

53. Proclamation of Governor Scott, December 22, 1871, Loose Papers, Legislative Proclamations, 1871, S.C.A.

54. *House Journal, 1871–1872*, p. 181.

55. *Acts and Joint Resolutions of the General Assembly of the State of South Carolina, 1871–1875*, XV, p. 49, cited hereafter as *Acts and Joint Resolutions*.

freeholders. Before the office of land commissioner was abolished, Henry Hayne had reported to the General Assembly in November, 1871, that 168 plantations comprising 92,641.6 acres had been bought by the commission.[56] Of this amount, the surveyor reported that by February, 1871, his office had already surveyed and divided 97 plantations into 1,992 small farms.[57]

The settlement of between 9,000 and 10,000 Negroes or approximately 2,000 families upon their own lands[58] by the

56. Purchase Book, Land Commissioner's Office; *Repts. and Resols., 1871–1872*, pp. 340–49, 387. The secretary of state reported in 1872 that 112,404.6 acres had been purchased by the Land Commission (*Repts. and Resols., 1872–1873*, p. 134). Appendix III includes a list of the number of acres purchased in each county.

57. B. F. Jackson to R. C. De Large, June 5, 1870; B. F. Jackson to R. C. De Large, February 23, 1871, Land Transfer File, 1866–1877. The tabular statement of Jackson is 1,803 farms, but it is in error. Upon checking Jackson's figures the total turns out to be 1,992 lots. Nearly half the land purchased by the Land Commission was located in the counties of Charleston, Colleton, Georgetown, and Beaufort. This gave rise to the familiar complaint that as usual the low country enjoyed a favored position (Letter from L. B. Johnson to Robert K. Scott, October 24, 1870, General Letters File, Sept.–Oct. 1870, S.C.A.). The Advisory Board, however, was justified in its preferential treatment of the low country, since that area contained the largest Negro population, the most plantations, and the lowest prices per acre. In the low country the size of the lots was small, following the pattern introduced in the Sea Islands by the Federal government. For example, 25 acres was the average size lot sold on the Greenwich and Cattle Bluff tracts in Charleston County, and on the Rushland tract in the same county the plots averaged around 10 acres. In general, lots in the up-country contained between 50 and 100 acres (Account of Sales A, Secretary of State's Office; Duplicate Certificates A, Land Commissioner, S.C.; Duplicate Certificates B, Secretary of State's Office; Duplicate Certificates C, Land Commissioner, S.C.; Duplicate Titles A, Secretary of State; Settlement Book, Vol. 3, Sinking Fund Commission, S.C.A.; *Repts. and Resols., 1872–1873*, pp. 154–222). Appendix III includes a map of the distribution of the land purchased by the commission and reproductions of the plats of the Greenwich and Bates tracts.

58. B. F. Jackson Report to H. H. Kimpton, February 23, 1871 (misfiled), H. H. Kimpton Financial Quarterly Report, 1870 Land Transfer File; B. F. Jackson to R. C. De Large, February 23, 1871. The number of settlers may have been greater, since Jackson appears to have made mistakes in addition in his tabular statements, but 2,000 families closely parallels the 1,992 farms surveyed by February, 1871.

beginning of 1871 was a significant accomplishment. Since the only way the Negroes knew to support themselves was by the cultivation of the land, the more thrifty and industrious Negroes eagerly embraced the opportunity extended to them. In fact, "in almost every county large numbers of landless and homeless citizens have to be turned away, disappointed. The lands not being sufficient to supply half the demand."[59] In most cases, Land Commission lands sold for less than was asked in the open market, and in any case the terms of purchase were more lenient than could be obtained through individual purchase. Most settlers, during their first year of occupancy, promptly paid the interest due on the land. Some earned enough from their crops to make a payment on the principal.[60] According to Hayne, if the price of cotton in 1870 had not declined, this number probably would have been greater.[61] But in 1871, although more plantations were being subdivided, very few Negroes settled on them.[62] Evidently, the corrupt practices of the past had overtaken the program. However, in 1872, when the Republican legislature committed itself to the continuance of the land reform program by transferring the duties of the land commissioner to the secretary of state, the chronic organizational defects of the commission's work were corrected and an honest administration under the direction of Francis L. Cardozo was guaranteed.

59. Benjamin F. Jackson to R. C. De Large, November 15, 1870, Drawer 51, Division of General Services, S.C. Record Center.

60. Account of Sales A, Secretary of State's Office; Settlement Book, Vol. 3, Sinking Fund Commission, S.C.A.

61. *Repts. and Resols., 1871–1872*, pp. 7–9.

62. Account of Sales A, Secretary of State's Office; Settlement Book, Vol. 3, Sinking Fund Commission. *See* p. 142 n. for annual returns of county agents.

CHAPTER V

The Transition

IT TOOK NO SEER to perceive that times were ominous in 1872. Corruption, having set in early, thickened as time went by. Louis F. Post, a New Yorker who served for a time in a minor clerical post in South Carolina, described the atmosphere at Columbia as one producing a peculiarly intoxicating effect, "just to breathe it made one feel like going out and picking a pocket."[1]

In 1872 the Republican machine appeared invincible; the Union Reform party had ceased to exist and in general the Conservatives were politically inactive. Although 1872 constituted the high water mark of post-war Republicanism, the party was split into two factions: Reformers and Regulars. A split had been noted sometime before the party convention in the summer of 1872. Although the effort to impeach Scott in December, 1871, had come to nothing, even administration newspapers, appalled by the revelation of fraud in all areas of state government, clamored for the election of honest men to the legislature. But when the nominating convention met in

1. Louis F. Post, "A Carpetbagger in South Carolina," *Journal of Negro History*, X (January, 1925), 27.

1872, pleas for reform within the ranks were ignored, and
Franklin J. Moses, Jr., an almost perfect example of the con-
ventional definition of a scalawag, was nominated for the
governorship.[2]

His father, Franklin Moses, Sr., had been elected chief justice of the South Carolina Supreme Court in 1868, and served
with distinction until his death in March, 1877.[3] A man of
ability, Moses, Sr., apparently maintained the respect of his
fellow South Carolinians all during Reconstruction. His son,
on the other hand, was held in the greatest contempt, being
accused of such vices as disloyalty, cowardice, greed, and lust
for power. At the beginning of the war he had been an ardent
secessionist and was said to have raised the Confederate flag
over Fort Sumter after Major Anderson surrendered. He was
secretary to Governor Pickens throughout the war and supported Johnson's Reconstruction policy in 1865–1866. Moses
was admitted to the bar in 1866 and during 1866 and 1867 was
editor of the *Sumter News*. With the passage of the Congressional Reconstruction Acts in 1867, he broke with his past
political affiliations and came out in his editorials in favor of
Radical Republicanism.[4]

Considered a renegade, he was dismissed from the editorship
of the *Sumter News*, but his conduct met with the immediate
approval of the Republicans and the Negroes. Under the Republican government he was to hold simultaneously the offices
of speaker of the House of Representatives, adjutant and in-
spector general, and trustee of the state university. In political
office he was thoroughly unscrupulous. During Moses's two

2. Simkins and Woody, pp. 126, 465–66.

3. *Ibid.*, pp. 142–43; Lillian A. Kibler, *Benjamin F. Perry: South Carolina
Unionist* (Durham: Duke University Press, 1946), p. 476.

4. Robert H. Woody, "Franklin J. Moses, Jr., Scalawag Governor of South
Carolina, 1872–74," *The North Carolina Historical Review*, X (April, 1933),
111–32; Simkins and Woody, p. 126.

terms as speaker, he issued fraudulent pay certificates and accepted bribes for favoring certain legislation. As adjutant general he misappropriated funds designated for the purchase of arms and ammunition for the militia. His personal life, as immoral as his political life, created a public scandal.[5]

It is no wonder that the nomination of Moses precipitated a break in the state party which coincided in time with the Liberal Republican movement on the national level. James L. Orr, former Democratic governor of South Carolina, withdrew from the Republican state convention and with him went about one-third of the delegates. Orr had been elected judge of the Eighth Judicial Circuit by the Republican legislature in September, 1868, but unlike the younger Moses, he was considered to be a man of ability and integrity. He had cast his lot with the Republican party during Reconstruction, believing it important for prominent white men of the state to identify themselves with the party in power. In that way, he reasoned, native white South Carolinians could control or at least temper the party's actions, expose corruption, and bring about reform.[6] When it became apparent to him that he could not control the party in the interest of conservatism—the nomination of Moses made this all too obvious—he bolted the party, taking many with him. The scrupulously honest Reuben Tomlinson was chosen to lead the Republican bolters as their nominee for governor on a separate state ticket.[7] The campaign produced strange political allies; among the prominent white bolters besides Orr and Tomlinson were D. T. Corbin, F. A. Sawyer, B. F. Whittemore, Timothy Hurley, and C. C. Bowen. Among the Negroes bolting the regulars were

5. *Ibid.*, pp. 126–27.
6. Anderson *Intelligencer*, April 7, 1870; *New York Times*, August 20, 1870; Charleston *News and Courier*, May 7, 1873; Kibler, p. 476; Simkins and Woody, p. 127.
7. Simkins and Woody, p. 466; Williamson, pp. 361, 397.

W. J. Whipper, S. A. Swails, Robert Smalls, R. C. De Large, and B. A. Boseman.[8] Although the bolters attacked the Republican administration, especially the abuses connected with finances, they made no alliance with the Democrats. The Democrats probably agreed with the sentiment stated in an editorial in *The Nation*: "Part of the opposition to the Scott and Moses gang means merely that the thieves have fallen out." Indeed, the Fairfield *Herald* could see no virtue in either Moses or Tomlinson. The former was a "scalawag who jumped into the arms of Radicalism when it first made its appearance," while Tomlinson was "a carpetbagger who was wafted South. . . ."[9] In any case, the Democrats refused to endorse the nominees of the bolters, and on election day, October 16, 1872, Moses carried the state with 69,838 votes, as compared with Tomlinson's 36,533.[10]

During the next two years, Governor Moses outdid his predecessor, Scott, in gross extravagance. He received bribes for approving measures of legislation, pardons, and official appointments.[11] It seems incongruous that in this setting of corrupt careers, prodigal expenditures, and notorious misrule, the Land Commission should blossom and reach its peak in sales, efficiency, and probity as an agency within the office of the secretary of state.

The causes for this transformation from irresponsibility to uprightness are manifold, yet there is one overriding factor. The Land Commission, having been impugned as "a gigantic

8. *The Nation*, October 10, 1872, p. 226; Simkins and Woody, p. 467; Williamson, p. 397.

9. *The Nation*, August 29, 1872, p. 130; Fairfield *Herald*, September 4, 1872. Williamson (pp. 396–97) considers the political campaign of 1872, although ostensibly between Reformers and Regulars, a fight between Republican factions standing on the same principles, the real issues being personal.

10. Simkins and Woody, pp. 466–68.

11. Governor Moses's Papers, *passim*, S.C.A.; *News and Courier*, August 31, 1874; Simkins and Woody, p. 474; Williamson, p. 332.

folly" by the report of the Joint Special Financial Investigating Committee, was denied further appropriations, and because of this, oddly enough, the experiment was salvaged. Since nothing remained in the treasury from former appropriations, there was nothing left to steal, and the Land Commission was thenceforth unencumbered by adventurers seeking booty. Moreover, by transferring the duties of the land commissioner to the secretary of state, the agency was relieved of mismanagement. Two honest men—Francis L. Cardozo and Henry E. Hayne—held the office of secretary of state during the remaining years of Reconstruction, and broadly speaking, the redemption of the experiment can be attributed to the efforts of these two Negro administrators.[12]

Cardozo had been officially connected with the Land Commission since its inception in 1869. It had been his responsibility as secretary of the Advisory Board to record all purchases. Rebuffed by other members of the board when he brought charges of corruption against C. P. Leslie, Cardozo resigned, but resumed his duties after Leslie's resignation had

12. It is difficult to make an accurate appraisal of the character of the Negroes who held office in South Carolina during Reconstruction. So often they are clouded in obscurity, or else so reviled by the Redeemers on the basis of their color, that to this day it is hard to differentiate between the good and the bad. As late as 1932 a South Carolina historian revealed his extreme personal distaste for Reconstruction Negro politicians in general, and Cardozo in particular. Yates Snowden wrote a blistering letter to his former student, Broadus Mitchell, concerning Francis Lewis Cardozo of Richmond Hill, New York, whom Mitchell had referred to Snowden for genealogical help. "It is a fair inference that he is *the son* of Francis L. Cardozo, graduate of the Univ. of Edinbro', a mulatto preacher, lawyer, sometime Secty of State and State Treas'r of S. C. during the 'years of good stealing.'" Snowden told Mitchell he could verify "Rev. Cardozo's stealing" by referring to Reynold's *History of Reconstruction in S. C., "passim*, but especially pp. 297 and 485" (Yates Snowden to Broadus Mitchell, February 9, 1932 (copy), Snowden Collection, Box 2, S.C.L.). He instructed Mitchell, "don't refer any more S.C. mulattoes to me, dear Broadus, I am in my 74th year and I confess I cannot see the joke" (*Ibid.*).

been secured in March, 1870.[13] He was not acting with the board during its most corrupt period, and he alone was untainted by scandal.[14] The records themselves indicate that Cardozo executed his duties well and brought renewed vigor to the original altruistic idea of providing land for the landless and homes for the homeless. He inherited an experiment eroded by fiscal irresponsibility, a staff of corrupt agents, and a mass of Land Commission records which were confused, conflicting, and generally incomprehensible. With the help of only two aides, Cardozo preserved the experiment, sustained and aided the settlers in their effort to own their own homesteads, introduced a plan of record management into the program,[15] and established a reputation as an administrator worthy of highest esteem.[16]

On March 1, 1872, Henry Hayne delivered the Land Commission records to Cardozo. Although the previous land commissioner had done something toward arranging the records of his agency, much remained to be done. Cardozo began by remedying organizational defects that had plagued the commission from its inception and had enabled its administrators to conceal their misappropriation of funds. He gathered proof that local county agents had collected payments from the settlers but had retained these sums for their own use. This evidence he placed before the legislature, and as a result an act was passed on March 13, 1872, stating that if fees collected by a county agent from settlers were not immediately

13. Advisory Board Minutes, October 30, 1869; March 1, 1870.
14. D. M. Porter to D. H. Chamberlain, June 6, 1870 (Porter's copy), Samuel Dibble Papers, Duke University; Simmons, p. 430; Sweat, *Journal of Negro History*, XLVI, p. 220.
15. Report of the Secretary of State to the General Assembly, *Repts. and Resols., 1872–1873*, pp. 48–50, 134–225.
16. Simmons, pp. 429–30; Sweat, pp. 220–31; Williamson, p. 147.

turned over to the secretary of state, "the same shall, in the aggregate be deducted from his salary."[17] Many agents refused to be chastened by the passage of this act, whereupon Cardozo removed them from office. To J. L. Woolley, the land agent in Edgefield, Cardozo wrote that he was dispensing with his and all other agents' services, "so as to administer the affairs of the Land Commission Department of my office as economically as possible."[18] Cardozo moved swiftly. By the end of May most agents had been removed; they were replaced by a single agent, J. E. Green, sergeant at arms of the State Senate. He was paid $100 a month plus expenses[19] to visit each tract in person and report to Cardozo the results of his investigations.[20] Until Green's report was received Cardozo possessed no accurate or detailed accounts of the true quality of the land purchased by the state, nor was he properly informed about the progress of settlement on the subdivided tracts. Green's report sustained in part the charges of the Financial Investigating Committee that the state in many instances had bought tracts of land at prices far above their actual value. These, he stated, remained unoccupied. Other tracts he extolled as containing some of the best land in the state, which after subdividing had been sold and settled upon immediately by the land-hungry Negroes.[21]

To Cardozo the significance of Green's report lay not only in its appraisal of the state-owned property, but also in the complaints of the Negroes stated therein. Although passionate in their desire to purchase land on the state's easy terms, the

17. *Acts and Joint Resolutions, 1871–1875*, XV, p. 239.
18. F. L. Cardozo to J. L. Woolley, May 25, 1872, Commission Letters, Secretary of State, 1870–1878, Letterbook, S.C.A.
19. Day Book A, Secretary of State Land Commission Office, S.C.A.
20. *Repts. and Resols., 1872–1873*, p. 49.
21. *Ibid.*, pp. 142–153.

Negroes made clear to Green their inability and unwilling-
ness to pay two or three times the value of the land, as was then
being charged by the state. Cardozo brought the complaints
of the Negroes to the attention of the board. The members
were cooperative and promptly passed a resolution on April
1, 1872, authorizing the secretary of state "to dispose of lands
of the state to settlers at their actual value, after making the
most careful inquiries to ascertain the same."[22] A few weeks
before the passage of this resolution, the legislature had shown
its concern for the welfare of the Land Commission settlers.
One provision of the act of March 13, 1872 (instructing the
sub-land-commissioners to turn over their funds to the secretary of state), specified that in every case where the sum of ten
dollars had been collected from a settler as a fee for title to the
property,[23] this amount was to be credited to his account as
part payment on the land.[24] Moreover, Cardozo rescinded the
part of the act of 1869 that required a settler to reside on the
tract three years before being eligible for a certificate of purchase. To each person who desired to purchase and could
begin payments on the principal, he gave a certificate.[25] These
concessions represented an acknowledgment of past wrongs
and seemed to reaffirm the belief that the Negro could become a self-supporting citizen.

Even more praiseworthy was Cardozo's attempt to reduce
the almost inextricable mass of Land Commission records to
a system of order and clarity. During his remaining ten months
as secretary of state, Cardozo with the aid of a clerk, Walter
R. Jones, prepared a mammoth report for the legislature. Car-

22. Minutes of the Advisory Board, April 1, 1872.
23. A requirement of the act of March 27, 1869.
24. *Acts and Joint Resolutions, 1871–1875*, XV, p. 239.
25. *Repts. and Resols., 1872–1873*, pp. 48–49.

dozo was impeded since only fragmentary reports concerning past accounts with settlers had been received from the county agents in office before their replacement by Green.[26] By assimilating, analyzing, and synthesizing all the miscellaneous reports of the treasurer, Advisory Board, financial agent, land commissioners, and county agents, and information from the certificates of purchase and deeds on file in his office, Cardozo published a comprehensive financial record of Land Commission transactions from its inception in October, 1869, through November 1, 1872.[27] This report, as submitted to the legislature, was to be consulted and built upon by Republican and Democratic administrations alike. Furthermore, the secretary of state had uncovered an additional 20,000 acres of Land Commission land hithertofore unreported. He estimated the total number of acres purchased by the commission at 112,-404.6.[28] Although he accounted for 20,000 acres more than his predecessor had reported, neither could account for $224,-620.44 of the $802,137.44 spent by the Land Commission.[29]

The year 1872 was obviously the Land Commission's year of transition—the experiment's original purpose was reestablished by the act of February, 1872, the act of March 13, 1872, the April resolution of the Advisory Board, the Green report, and, most significant of all, Cardozo's report to the legislature. As a result of these reforms, by the fall of 1872 at least 5,008 families—approximately 3,000 more families than in 1871—

26. Accounts of settlement were received from only 21 of the 28 county agents, and their returns accounted for only 1,047 families in residence by the fall of 1872 (Account of Sales A, Secretary of State's Office, Settlement Book, Vol. 3, S.C.A.).

27. *Repts. and Resols., 1872–1873*, pp. 48–50, 134–225.

28. *Ibid.*, p. 134. Appendix III includes Cardozo's statement of the number of acres purchased in each county.

29. *Repts. and Resols., 1872–1873*, p. 135.

had settled on Land Commission tracts.[30] The year of transition demonstrated that under the direction of on honest, energetic, and capable administrator the experiment could be redeemed and the "gigantic folly" rendered a misnomer.

Cardozo was elected state treasurer in 1872; his successor as secretary of state carried on the comprehensive reform he had begun. Henry Hayne's appointment as land commissioner had served a worthwhile purpose in promoting the political aspirations of a man of integrity who became secretary of state in 1872, thus assuming the guardianship of the Land Department. Hayne and Cardozo had much in common—both were mulattoes, both were honest and efficient men who had risen to important official positions during Reconstruction, and both had had previous experience in Land Commission affairs. Hayne had deep regard for Cardozo and sought to implement the policies inaugurated by him. They differed, however, in one critical respect: Cardozo was more compassionate in his dealings with the settlers. He, as stated elsewhere, issued certificates to all desiring to purchase without requiring a period of residency, and often extended the deadline for pay-

30. The total 5,008 is the number of certificates of purchase issued by November, 1872; 851 certificates of purchase had been issued by September, 1872 (Duplicate Titles A, Secretary of State; Duplicate Certificate B, Secretary of State's Office) to settlers whose names appear before 1872 in the partial returns of the county agents (Accounts of Sales A, Secretary of State's Office; Settlement Book, Vol. 3; *Repts. and Resols., 1872–1873*, pp. 154–222). Of the remaining 4,157 certificates issued by Cardozo (Loose Certificates of Purchase, Drawers 3, 7, 11, 15, 16, 51, Division of General Services, S. C. Record Center), probably many were in residence before 1872 but were not included in the county agents' returns. Nevertheless, it is not unreasonable to assume that the majority of certificates were issued to new settlers under Cardozo's liberal policy of issuing them to anyone desiring to purchase without requiring three years' residence. For instance, although the county agents' returns are meagre they indicate an increasing number of settlers took up lots in 1872. Twenty-six settlers are recorded in 1869; 359 more in 1870; only 156 were added in 1871; whereas 506 settled in 1872 (Accounts of Sales A, Secretary of State's Office; Settlement Book, Vol. 3). Furthermore, all 506 families recorded as taking up residence in 1872 received certificates of purchase that year.

ments for those who found it a hardship to comply with the
terms of purchase; Hayne was less patient. As early as the
spring of 1873 Hayne instructed trial justices to eject settlers
who had delayed making payment on their tracts, to make
room for those of "wiser economy and those of more increasing industry who could become owners of the land."[31]
Moreover, he reverted to the former three-year residence requirement and payment of interest as prerequisites for ac-
quiring certificates of purchase. Negro landholders soon voiced
their opposition to Hayne's stricter management of the program, echoing the complaints of white landowners that exces-
sive and oppressive taxation instituted by those who paid
little or no taxes[32] prevented them from complying with the
terms of purchase. In addition, the panic of 1873, although
not severe in South Carolina, had resulted in the lowering of
cotton prices in 1874.[33] Negroes, South Carolina's poorest citizens, were hardest pressed. They had little or no savings, and
in the face of falling cotton prices they had little chance of
accumulating a surplus.

Agrarian protests came to a climax in 1874, when the financial crisis had depressed the value of all agricultural products.
Negroes, as well as whites, clamored for relief. The Republican legislature, in recognition of Negro voting strength and
conscious that this was an election year, attempted to alleviate some of the causes of Negro discontent. By joint resolution, payments of installments and interest due on commission lands were postponed until December, 1874,[34] that is,
until after the crops had been harvested and after the election

31. Letter from Henry Hayne to I. B. Sherman, March 23, 1873; Henry
Hayne to A. A. Gantt, March 24, 1873; Henry Hayne to Simeon Young, May
2, 1873, Commission Letters, Secretary of State, 1870–1878, Letterbook.
32. *Proceedings of the Taxpayers' Convention, 1871*, p. 21.
33. Williamson, p. 168.
34. *Acts and Joint Resolutions, 1871–1875*, XV, p. 804.

returns had been tallied. Hayne had no alternative but to submit to this reprieve, but he registered his disapproval in his report to the legislature, complaining that their tampering with his land policies had resulted in considerably fewer payments than he had anticipated. Many homesteaders, Hayne insinuated, could have made their payments but had taken advantage of the resolution.[35] The secretary of state made it known that after December, 1874, he would resume his former policy and the settlers would "be required to pay the deficiency this winter." He hoped, moreover, that "the collections will be so augmented as to go far toward reimbursing the State for the amount originally expended."[36]

Hayne was overly optimistic; the state never was, nor ever could be, fully reimbursed. Cardozo had reported that over $224,000 of Land Commission funds had been drained away by fraud and was totally unaccounted for; furthermore, the state could never recover the excessive sums it had paid for some tracts, since by the resolution of the Advisory Board the Land Commission had agreed to sell the tracts to the homesteaders at the actual value of the land. Nevertheless, the introduction by Cardozo and Hayne of a more accurate accounting system had greatly reduced the expense of collecting from the settlers, thereby augmenting the treasury. Under the former method of collection, salaries and expenses of local agents often amounted to as much as (or in some instances, more than) the sums obtained from the Negroes.[37] Green, named by Cardozo to be general agent, retained his position during Hayne's tenure in office. The cost, including Green's salary of $100 a month plus travel expenses, amounted to less

35. *Repts. and Resols., 1874–1875*, p. 069.
36. *Ibid.*
37. *Repts. and Resols., 1874–1875*, p. 069.

than 8 per cent of the total collections from the settlers.[38] The general agent in his travels around the state proved to be a real asset to Hayne. He discovered in some cases that the state was charging the settlers far less than the actual value of the land, whereupon Hayne promptly increased the prices of these lots thereby increasing the financial returns. In addition, he reported that some tracts were still unsurveyed as late as 1874. For example, although only one tract—the Bigger plantation—had been purchased in Clarendon County,[39] five years had passed, and by 1874 this tract had not yet been correctly surveyed. Hayne, exasperated at Jackson's delay, demanded of his surveyor that all surveys be completed at once. After more delay, Hayne, his patience at an end, employed local surveyors to complete the subdivision of the remaining tracts.[40]

During Hayne's administration it appeared that the South Carolina Land Commission might, after all, be a success. Although Hayne had overestimated his ability in promising to convert the experiment into a profit-making venture for the state, he had made great strides in establishing the Negroes as landowners and in giving them a stake in the future of the state. Important as suffrage had been to the freedmen during Reconstruction, land and education would become more significant, more practical, and more tangible means of social advancement in the post-Reconstruction era. By 1876 Hayne estimated that 14,000 families[41] or approximately 70,000 persons had participated in the experiment. This number is a

38. Day Book A, pp. 4–35, S.C.A.
39. Purchase Book, Land Commissioner's Office, November 27, 1869.
40. Letter from Henry Hayne to J. C. Burgess, May 13, 1874, Commission Letters, Secretary of State, 1870–1878, Letterbook. There are 22 letters in all written by Hayne concerning the employment of local surveyors (*Ibid*).
41. *See* Appendix I.

significant fraction of the estimated total nonwhite population
of South Carolina, which in 1870 had been 415,814, increasing to 604,332 in 1880.[42] Approximately 14 per cent of that
population, had benefited directly from the establishment of
the commission.

Although the Negroes dominated the experiment from the
beginning, some whites acquired their first parcel of land
through the commission. The tracts were not segregated; in
the up-country counties of Chester, Oconee, and Greenville
especially, Negroes and whites lived side by side on the same
tract.[43] For instance, on the Lewis tract in Oconee County six
deeds had been issued to white men, seven to black men, and
one to a mulatto. On the same tract, of the 19 holders of certificates of purchase still in residence in 1880, four were white,
two were mulatto, and 13 were black. On the Yocum tract in
Chester County, two white families held land bordering on a
Negro homestead. In Greenville, of eight deed holders on the
Cleaveland tract, six were white and two were black, and certificates of purchase had been issued to an additional eight
white men and five black men.[44] One particularly enterprising
white man, John D. Harrison, and his wife Sally, had increased

42. Julian Petty, *Growth and Distribution of Population in South Carolina*,
Industrial Development Committee of the State Council of Defense, Bulletin
11 (Columbia, 1943), p. 28. The increase in number of Negroes in South Carolina between 1870 and 1880 is not as large as it appears in the statistics. The
census of 1870 is inadequate because of its under-enumeration of Southern
Negroes (Allen W. Trelease, "Who Were the Scalawags?" *Journal of Southern
History*, XXIX [November, 1963], 451, citing Francis A. Walker, "Statistics of
the Colored Race in the United States," American Statistical Association,
Publications, 11 [1890], 95–99, 106).
43. Public Land Plats Book I, 1857, 1869–1899, 1909, 1918, *passim*; U. S.
Census Records, State of South Carolina, 1880 Population Schedules (Abbeville-
York), Microfilm Publications, 27 reels, cited hereafter as *S. C. Census, 1880.*
44. *Ibid.*; See also Appendix II. The census returns of 1880 differentiate between black and mulatto in designating race (*S. C. Census, 1880*).

their Land Commission holdings in Fairfield County from 36 acres in 1871 to 733 acres by 1889.[45]

Ownership of land by the South Carolina freedmen and poor whites, only a dream at the end of the Civil War, had become a reality for some midway through Reconstruction. Through the experiment, the Negro appeared to have become a full-fledged participant in society—citizen, voter, officeholder, and landowner. The question remained as to whether or not the experiment would prove equal to the challenges of the future or if, instead, it would be drowned in the floodstream of reaction.

45. Office Secretary of State, Duplicate Titles A, 1872–1880; Duplicate Titles B, 1880–1887; Duplicate Titles C, 1887–1924, S.C.A. The Harrisons were either related to or were the original owners of the Harrison tract in Fairfield County, because in 1888 John D. Harrison received a deed for four acres of the burying plot of the Harrison family (Duplicate Titles C, State of South Carolina, p. 6).

CHAPTER VI

The Counter Revolution

THE TRIUMPH WAS SHORT-LIVED. By 1876 the land experiment, handicapped by its unsavory past, was meeting with renewed opposition.

The gubernatorial campaign of 1874 was similar to that of 1872 in that a Republican faction demanding immediate reforms separated from the "Regulars," but in this election, unlike that of 1872, the "Reformers," or "Independents," won the support of the "Conservatives" (Democrats). When the Republicans convened at Columbia there was no thought of renominating the "scalawag" Moses. Everyone, including the stalwarts, conceded that reform was essential to the party's continued existence. Daniel H. Chamberlain won the nomination over John T. Green, and the incumbent lieutenant governor, R. H. Gleaves, was renominated over Martin R. Delany.[1] The Reformers bolted the convention, disappointed over the defeat of Green and Delany and appalled by the nomination of Chamberlain, a man closely identified with the

1. *News and Courier*, September 11, 14, 1874; Simkins and Woody, pp. 470–71.

Land Commission scandals and other fraudulent transactions committed during the Scott administration. In fact, the Charleston *News and Courier* declared that the former attorney general "is as deep in the mud as Moses is in the mire. . . ."[2]

An Independent Republican state convention was held in Charleston, and, although adopting the platform of the Regulars, nominated John T. Green and Martin R. Delany, the candidates defeated at the Regular convention. Green, a native of South Carolina, had served the people well as judge of the third circuit. His running mate, Martin R. Delany, a Virginia-born Negro, well-educated and well-traveled, had won the respect of both races as an agent of the Freedmen's Bureau. In their bid for political office on the Independent Republican ticket, Green and Delany won the endorsement of the Conservatives. Although they were defeated by Chamberlain and the Regulars, the Independents had succeeded in bringing about increased white participation in the election. The vote, 68,818 to 80,403, was the largest cast since 1868.[3]

As Governor, Chamberlain surprised the Independents as well as some of his "stalwart" supporters who had given only lip service to a Republican platform of reform. By continuous and urgent messages to the legislature, Chamberlain demonstrated that virtue and morality were not the monopolies of a single faction or a single party. Among his achievements were the reduction of taxes, the appointment of more capable county officials, and the installation of an economical and efficient state government. During the legislative session of 1875 he handed down nineteen vetoes. His attempt to undo the

2. Charleston *News and Courier*, August 28, 1874.

3. *Ibid.*, October 5, 1874; Simkins and Woody, pp. 470–473; Williamson, pp. 28, 353–354, 365.

gross extravagance of his predecessors met with vigorous opposition among the Radicals in the legislature, led by Robert
Elliott, speaker of the House, C. C. Bowen, B. F. Whittemore,
and W. J. Whipper. To the chagrin of the Radicals the nineteen vetoes could not be overridden; the Conservatives and
Independents had united to sustain Chamberlain.[4]

Reforms during Chamberlain's administration activated
further reform. The irrepressible C. P. Leslie, sensing the
change and haunted by the fear of being submerged under a
reforming wave, bobbed up as an independent. Now a member of the House from Barnwell, Leslie came forth in the
character of a reformer championing tax reform. He proclaimed that the acute suffering of merchants and farmers
throughout the state made it essential to reduce taxes. "A
larger tax than eleven mills," he warned his colleagues, "could
not be passed."[5] Judge Alfred Aldrich (also of Barnwell),
doubtful of Leslie's true conversion, signed an affidavit in
December, 1875, charging C. P. Leslie, ex-land commissioner,
with a breach of trust with fraudulent intent because of his
failure to account for about $225,000 of state money during
his administration.[6] Aldrich himself was somewhat given to
histrionics. At the fall term of the circuit court in Barnwell in
1867, Judge Aldrich had adjourned the court rather than obey
an order of General Canby of the Second Military District
making Negroes eligible for jury duty. Aldrich at that time
had announced: "Gentlemen of the jury, for the present fare-
well; but if God spares my life, I will yet preside in this court,
a South Carolina judge whose ermine is unstained. . . . Mr.
Sheriff, let the court stand adjourned while the voice of jus-

4. Walter Allen, *Governor Chamberlain's Administration in South Carolina*
(New York, 1888), *passim*; *News and Courier*, July 6, 1876; Simkins and Woody,
pp. 474–77.

5. *News and Courier*, December 10, 1875.

6. Fairfield *Herald*, February 21, 1876; *Repts. and Resols., 1875–1876*, p. 1165.

tice is stifled!'"[7] Considering its source, Aldrich's affidavit would probably have been ignored had it not been for Leslie's persistence.

Leslie demanded once again that an investigation be undertaken, but this time by a committee composed of Democratic members of the House. And once again his motives are suspect. Was it merely a sham to gratify his continuous hunger for publicity even if it brought notoriety in its wake, or was Leslie, tormented by conscience, seeking self-abasement? Whatever his personal reasons, he stated publicly: "If investigated by Republicans, the Democrats would insist I have been whitewashed, thus only an investigation conducted by Democrats would be sufficient to clear my name."[8] It is more than likely that Leslie, although courting an investigation, felt he had more to fear from his own party—which might be seeking revenge for his defection—than from the Democrats.

In January, 1876, the speaker of the House appointed three Democrats—Livingston of Oconee, Wallace of Union, and Johnson of Marion—to conduct the probe.[9] The Democrats, rejoicing in their good fortune, expanded their inquiry to include all the transactions of the ex-land commissioner. Leslie thereupon grumbled, insisting that the committee was charged only with the investigation of the "alleged" deficiency of $225,000. Revenge, however, was sweet for the Republicans, and the House speaker denied Leslie's motion to limit the investigation, ruling that the committee had a right under Leslie's own resolution to probe any matters upon which the

7. Yates Snowden, *History of South Carolina* (New York: The Lewis Publishing Company, 1920), II, 965 n. Aldrich after Reconstruction presided in court, having been elected judge of the second circuit in 1878 (*House Journal 1877–1878*, p. 480).

8. *News and Courier*, January 31, 1876.

9. *Repts. and Resols., 1875–1876*, p. 1165; *News and Courier*, January 31, 1876.

accusation of breach of trust could be predicated.[10] The editor
of the Charleston *News and Courier* acidly commented, "Play-
ing hare is a very pretty game, and a profitable one under certain restrictions, but it loses rapidly in interest—to the hare
—as soon as the dogs get in earnest."[11]

If the hare had been the only victim when the dogs stalked
in earnest, nothing would have been lost except the time spent
in hammering out a report that was more than 100 pages
long.[12] It reiterated old charges and time-worn testimony and
brought nothing new to light; but in raking up the past the
investigators heaped further discredit on the Land Commission and neglected entirely to mention the restorative work
of the past four years. Contributing to the distorted picture of
the land experiment was none other than the chief executive.

Governor Chamberlain was a witness called to testify before
the House committee of 1876. He was asked to evaluate the
work of the Land Commission. Chamberlain as leader of the
reform movement could not straddle the issue; he had to dis-
associate himself from the taint of corruption that clung to
him because of his serving as a member of the Advisory Board.
He denied ever having acted carelessly or dishonestly while
on the Advisory Board and then he proceeded to lash out at
the experiment. "The whole theory of the Land Commission
was an enormous mistake," he told the committee.[13] Many
purchases were improper, but upon whom the blame should
rest he could not say. "In fact, the ease with which . . . frauds
could have been committed, while every member of the Board

10. *News and Courier*, February 5, 1876.
11. February 8, 1876.
12. Report of the House Special Committee to Investigate Charge of Breach
of Trust Against C. P. Leslie, ex-land commissioner, *Repts. and Resols.*, 1875–
1876, pp. 1159–1261.
13. *Ibid.*, p. 1219.

might have been anxious to have done his duty, was one of the most remarkable features of the Land Commission."[14]

The results of the investigation were largely negative. The committee of 1876, like that of 1871, found Leslie guilty as charged,[15] but it appeared that justice could not be obtained under even so reforming a Republican administrator as Chamberlain. Leslie, although found guilty of being a bribe-giver and bribe-taker by two separate investigating committees, was not brought to justice. According to one Democratic newspaper:

> There has been so much sham investigation, so much sham prosecution, so many sham trials of public thieves, and there are so many of the plunderers now free who ought to be in the penitentiary, that there is little ground to believe that Leslie will ever be held to answer for his crimes. Parker, Scott, Neagle, and Kimpton, to say nothing of lesser lights, such as defaulting county officers, have all enjoyed the fullest freedom from annoyance on account of their stealings, and we have but little idea that Leslie will ever be troubled.[16]

Moreover, the labors of the committee and the damaging testimony by Chamberlain were widely circulated in the newspapers. Since no attention was directed toward the good accomplished in the interval, South Carolinians remained unaware of the accomplishments since 1872 and were made to recall only the Land Commission's scandalous past.

Unfortunately for those who worked so diligently to wreathe the experiment in success, and for those who directly benefited from it, time was running out. Within the year, Reconstruction in South Carolina was to end.

14. *Ibid.*, pp. 1219–21.
15. *News and Courier*, April 15, 1876.
16. Fairfield *Herald*, April 26, 1876.

66666666666

2

Why was Chamberlain, the reforming Republican governor, not re-elected in 1876? Although he had come into office with a reputation not untarnished by corruption, his actions as governor had won for him the approval and endorsement of a large portion of the press and populace. Since there had been no Democratic organization worthy of the name after the 1868 campaign, some former Democrats advocated a fusion of the native whites with the better elements of the Republican party to support Chamberlain for re-election. On the other hand, opposition to the fusionists' or cooperationists' plan was expressed by those favoring a straightout Democratic ticket in 1876 with no thought of an alliance with the Republicans.[17] The editor of the *News and Courier*, a staunch supporter of Chamberlain and his reforms, gave his own objections to the scheme of the "straightouters." The colored majority was between 20,000 and 30,000, and the solid Negro bloc vote combined with the power to obtain Federal troops at any time made it extremely unlikely that the incumbent could be defeated except through armed force. Furthermore, since Chamberlain had made such a strong record as a reformer, all the people of the state could rest assured that he was a safe candidate.[18] Many historians since John Reynolds have held that until July, 1876, the sentiment for fusionism prevailed and that two incidents in particular, occurring in 1876, worked for the Straightouters, paving the way for a solid Democratic ticket. Although it does not lie within the scope of this study to discuss in detail the dramatic campaign of

17. Simkins and Woody, pp. 480–81.
18. *News and Courier*, May 9, 1876.

1876, some details of it are pertinent to the continuity of the narrative.[19]

The first incident, involving chiefly the issue of Republican corruption, began in December, 1875, with the election of W. J. Whipper, a Negro, and the "scalawag" Franklin J. Moses, Jr., as circuit judges by the Radical legislature. Both men had been repeatedly charged with corruption. Chamberlain's refusal to sign their commissions did not prevent the Straightouters from citing this as an example of continued Republican corruption. However, it has been said, the second incident—the Hamburg riot, involving the more important issue of race—was what made certain the rejection of Chamberlain. On July 4, 1876, two white men on their way home to Edgefield tried to drive their carriage through Hamburg, but Negro militiamen parading on the main street refused to allow the carriage to proceed. After a long delay, the Edgefield men were allowed to continue, but the matter did not end there. A band of armed white men came to Hamburg to demand that the black militia surrender its weapons. Firing began between the Negroes and whites and ended with the deaths of about

19. For accounts of this election see John Schreiner Reynolds, *Reconstruction in South Carolina* (Columbia, 1905); Simkins and Woody, *South Carolina During Reconstruction* (Chapel Hill, 1932); William A. Sheppard, *Red Shirts Remembered: Southern Brigadiers of Reconstruction Period* (Atlanta, 1940); Alruthus Ambush Taylor, *The Negro in South Carolina during the Reconstruction* (Washington, 1924); Henry Tazewell Thompson, *Ousting the Carpetbagger from South Carolina* (Columbia, 1926); Alfred Brockenbrough Williams, *Hampton and His Red Shirts: South Carolina's Deliverance in 1876* (Columbia, 1935); Edward L. Wells, *Hampton and Reconstruction* (Columbia, 1907); Walter Allen, *Governor Chamberlain's Administration in South Carolina* (New York, 1888); *Recent Election in South Carolina: Testimony Taken by the Select Committee on the Recent Election in South Carolina* (House Miscellaneous Documents, 44th Congress, 2nd Session, No. 31); *South Carolina in 1876: Testimony as to the Denial of the Elective Franchise in South Carolina at the Elections of 1875 and 1876*, 3 vols. (Senate Miscellaneous Documents, 44th Congress, 2nd Session, No. 48).

twenty-five militiamen. The incident might not have taken a political turn except for Chamberlain's action in writing President Grant that Federal troops might be needed in the future to quell riots during the political campaign. Thereafter, moderate voices were lost amidst the shouts of those vilifying a regime kept in power by Federal troops and bayonets.[20]

These two incidents may have been the immediate causes for the withdrawal of support from Chamberlain, but deeper underlying causes probably made the year 1876 the time for a trial of Democratic strength and the year 1877 the year of Redemption. The reaction to the election of Moses and Whipper as circuit judges and the riots at Hamburg were symptoms rather than causes of popular unrest. What fiery elements had collected in South Carolina during eight years of Republican rule, and what spark set them ablaze in 1876? What circumstances within the body politic made it possible for a Democratic show of strength to be successful in 1876, when opposition to the Reconstruction government expressed in the Union Reform party of 1870, the Bolters of 1872, the Independents of 1874, the Taxpayers' Conventions of 1871 and 1874, as well as the Ku Klux Klan activities had all met with failure?

To begin with, the strength and popularity of the fusionist movement of 1876 had probably been exaggerated. The cooperationists, it seems, were for the most part Charleston businessmen, who were enjoying prosperity for the first time since the beginning of the war. This group doubted that the existing situation could be bettered by a change in party rule. Others favored fusionism because they had come to respect Chamberlain for his bipartisanship. Letters written to Chamberlain praised him for defying the Radical leaders by appoint-

20. *Ibid.*; George B. Tindall, *South Carolina Negroes, 1877–1900* (Columbia: University of South Carolina Press, 1952), pp. 11–12.

ing the most capable men to office irrespective of party affiliation.[21] The size of these two groups was probably small in proportion to the number of white voters in the state. No doubt it was the conspicuous position of the leading proponent of fusionism that made the number of its adherents, its energy, and its popular appeal appear greater than they were. Francis P. Dawson, an Englishman who had served in the Confederate army, remained in Charleston after the war as publisher, with Bartholomew Riordon, of the Charleston *News*. In 1873 they had purchased the *Courier* and consolidated it with the *News*. Captain Dawson, then only 33 years old, became editor of the strongest and most widely circulated daily newspaper in the state.[22] During the election year Dawson monopolized the news, presenting persuasive arguments to bolster Chamberlain as the logical candidate for re-election.[23] Although many Democrats subscribed to the Charleston *News and Courier*, presumably few endorsed Dawson's candidate.

During Reconstruction in South Carolina, although life went on and adjustments were made to the existing regime, few whites had joined the Republican party. And most of the converts resided in the up-country[24] in such counties as Spartanburg, York, and Oconee. What is striking in studying the history of the Land Commission, or for that matter any other aspect of Reconstruction government, is the withdrawal of the majority of native whites from the body politic. This majority

21. Governor Chamberlain's Papers, *passim*, S.C.A.; Greenville *Enterprise and Mountaineer*, February 16, 1876; Kibler, pp. 483–84.

22. Herbert Ravenel Sass, *Outspoken: 150 Years of the News and Courier* (Columbia: University of South Carolina Press, 1953), pp. 38–40.

23. *News and Courier*, January–August 16, 1876, *passim*. Nevertheless, after Hampton's nomination by the Democratic convention, Dawson shifted the support of his paper to Hampton. He wrote that the *News and Courier* "will do its part to defeat the Radicals, one and all, and to elect the Democratic candidates. . ." (*News and Courier*, August 17, 1876).

24. *Ku Klux Conspiracy, S. C.*, III, pp. 5, 56, 196, 208, 247 and 738.

simply remained aloof from the new regime and, on the whole, yielded little while awaiting the propitious moment to restore the old order patterned on the legends of the "Old South" and the newer memory of the "lost cause." When new leadership appeared, proclaiming a potent doctrine and advocating new methods, they would be ready to seize power.

In the meantime, since the period was one of serious economic dislocation, most energies were probably absorbed in the necessary reality of daily living. Although on the surface things seemed peaceable enough, the whites managed to demonstrate hostility toward the Reconstruction government in quiet ways. What has been so often considered Democratic apathy in abstaining from voting and from reorganizing the Democratic party after its rout in 1868,[25] was probably an indication of the Democrats' implacable hostility toward the Reconstruction administration. While awaiting the moment to "sweep the Black Republican party out of existence,"[26] the Democrats refused to accord the Republican administration any official recognition. If seen in this light, political inaction probably reflected passive resistance to a government so entrenched by the aid of Negro votes that it could be dislodged only through the intimidation of these voters—a course the Democrats knew to be exceedingly dangerous as long as the Federal government might intervene.

There were, of course, some Democrats who refused to yield to the inevitable and took an early stand against the Republican regime to begin the long hard pull toward Redemption. During the period 1868–1874, although their cries for reform never succeeded in rallying enough support to uproot the Radical regime, their pleas for deliverance from corrupt rule

25. Kibler, pp. 476–77; Simkins and Woody, pp. 467–68; Trelease, *Journal of Southern History*, XXIX, 453.
26. Columbia *Phoenix*, July 3, 1867.

attracted such diverse elements as the rabid white supremacists, the true Conservatives, and all the "good" South Carolinians repelled by the moral bankruptcy of the state. The
inauguration of the Chamberlain administration on a platform of reform seriously threatened the continued existence
of this opposition. Defections did occur. Charleston businessmen, won over by prosperous times, followed Chamberlain's
leadership; others wavered. Bold new leadership, new methods, and an effective doctrine were essential to prevent further
defections to Chamberlain.

Martin W. Gary, "the Bald Eagle of Edgefield," rose to the
occasion. Gary not only provided the new leadership but also
replaced the relatively mild doctrine of reform with the more
potent one of racial superiority which succeeded in reuniting
the white opposition. With the whites united, enough energy
could be generated to convert general frustrations into a spe-
cific commitment to overthrow Republican rule. With a growing sense of power, the Democratic party was reorganized in
January, 1876, and a plan for the campaign of 1876 was formulated.[27] To succeed, the Democrats needed—in addition to
energy and resoluteness—the right moment, a moment when
the Republicans did not have or could not exercise the will
to resist the overthrow of their party. All these requirements
seemed to coincide in 1876. Exceptional incompetence, if not
complete moral and financial bankruptcy on the part of the
Reconstruction government, had produced a setting in South
Carolina receptive to change, and a special set of circumstances
within the Republican party diminished its capacity to sur-
vive. In this light the election of 1876 can best be understood
as a counter-revolution.[28]

27. Simkins and Woody, pp. 480–82; Kibler, p. 486; Williamson, pp. 405–06.
28. Hampton M. Jarrell, *Wade Hampton and the Negro: The Road Not
Taken* (Columbia: University of South Carolina Press, 1949), p. 41.

Chamberlain's reforms had probably accentuated and per-
petuated dissatisfaction with the existing governmental institutions. The investigations of fraud undertaken during the
period 1874–1876, and in particular the Land Commission
reinvestigation of 1876, had further discredited the prevailing
order in the eyes of the white populace. At the same time,
Chamberlain, as the leader of his party, ceased to perform his
primary function of maintaining party unity. The Republican
party, although split into two factions since the election of
1872, had not disintegrated earlier because in 1872 Moses had
been the representative of the dominant wing of the party.
After that election the Reformers had no alternative but to
return to work within the party. Chamberlain, however, did
not work for unity; in fact, he did just the opposite. He ac-
corded official recognition to the split within his party by
breaking with the Radical leaders of the majority wing and
personally assuming leadership of the minority group. While
the Republicans were absorbed with intra-party battles, their
effective control of the state was being loosened.

Consequently, in 1876 the Democrats, exploiting the dis-
ruption in the ranks of the Republican party, seized the initiative. Under the leadership of Martin W. Gary and M. C.
Butler, a straightout policy was advocated shunning any alliance with the Republicans. The timing was perfect. Fusion
had lost its appeal after Republican internal weaknesses had
been exposed, and a Democratic victory seemed possible. Although Gary and M. C. Butler pioneered the Straightout
movement, the Democratic nomination for governor went to
Wade Hampton, the Confederate war hero and owner of large
plantations in South Carolina and Mississippi. The Democrats
looked to him to endow the campaign with dignity and sta-
bility, and, if elected, to restore the state to its days of past
glory. Whereas Hampton and his moderate followers advo-

cated a vigorous but non-violent campaign, it was Gary and the more extremist elements—those willing to use force—who spearheaded the movement. Gary's plan, based upon the so-called "Mississippi plan" of the previous year, provided for Democratic rifle clubs to be established in each county. Each captain of the county organization was to see that his men were provided with "at least 30 rounds of ammunition." Members were to attend, armed and in great numbers, every Republican political meeting in their county, harassing the Republican speakers and frightening the Negro audiences. In addition to the display of arms, Gary's plan called for the use of force if necessary.

> Every Democrat must feel himself honor bound to control the vote of at least one negro, by intimidation, purchase, keeping him away from the polls, or as each individual may determine he may best accomplish it . . . . Never threaten a man individually. If he deserves to be threatened, the necessities of the times require he should die. A dead Radical is very harmless—a threatened Radical or one driven off by threats from the scene of his operations is often very troublesome, sometimes dangerous and always vindictive.[29]

Though the section concerning the "dead Radical" was deleted from the papers distributed over the state, these instructions were nevertheless verbally circulated to the various county clubs.

The Republican leaders were no match for the Democrats in the ensuing election. They renominated Chamberlain, but they were on the defensive. Many Republicans either retired voluntarily or were intimidated into passivity by the exertions of the rifle clubs; Chamberlain probably did not have more

29. MS "The Plan for Campaign," Martin Witherspoon Gary Papers, S.C.L.

than 500 white supporters other than his officeholders.[30] The Negroes—the bulk of the Republican vote in the state—appeared to stand alone, and it looked as if the Federal government did not plan to intervene in their behalf. As the campaign conducted by the Gary forces became more bitter and violent, Hampton and the Democratic executive committee warned the rifle clubs not to commit any acts that might give Chamberlain an excuse to call for Federal troops and thereby bring about the defeat of the Democrats. Meanwhile, Hampton and his more moderate followers concentrated their efforts on winning the Negroes over to the Democratic party by persuasion rather than by force.[31]

As early as 1865 Wade Hampton had sought a way to give newly freed slaves the opportunity to vote without endangering the political control of the whites. Thus in 1867 he had proposed limited suffrage based on education and ownership of property, qualifications that would apply to Negro and white alike. During his campaign speeches Hampton went further by pledging to the Negroes that "not one single right enjoyed by colored people today shall be taken from them. They shall be the equal under the law of any man in South Carolina."[32] In this manner he hoped to allay the Negroes' fears that the Democrats, once in power, would suppress their rights. Many moderates, in agreement with Hampton, tried to convince the Negroes of their sincerity, hoping thereby to split the black vote without using force.

30. W. J. Mixson to Chamberlain, September 27, 1876; Robert E. Evans to Chamberlain, September 30, 1876, Governor Chamberlain's Papers, S.C.A.; Simkins and Woody, pp. 499–509.

31. Jarrell, pp. 58–85; McKitrick, pp. 247–48.

32. Wade Hampton to James Conner, August 1, 1867, James Conner Papers, South Carolina Historical Society, Charleston; MS "Free Men, Free Ballots, Free Schools: The Pledge of General Wade Hampton to the Colored People of South Carolina," Wade Hampton Papers, S.C.L.

Benjamin F. Perry, who had been President Johnson's provisional governor in 1865, reminded the Negroes that it was not the Republicans but rather the state convention of 1865, representing all the slaveholders of the state, and the ratification of the Thirteenth Amendment by the state legislature that had abolished slavery in South Carolina.[33] In another address he reminded them of their need for Hampton's protection to act as a buffer between them and the wrath of the more extreme white elements, since their Republican benefactors appeared to have deserted them and their cause. "You must have a Governor who will protect you and not run away when tumults and riots occur. General Wade Hampton will make you that Governor, and he has pledged his solemn word to enforce the laws and see justice done to all alike without regard to race and color. . . ."[34]

Nevertheless, it was difficult to spur Negroes on to support a party whose leaders merely promised not to undo what had already been done for them by the Republicans, especially since it was evident that perhaps the majority of Hampton's party disagreed with his moderate approach.[35] A small number of Negroes did become Hampton Democrats, including some who had benefited directly from the Land Commission. According to B. S. Rivers, a settler on the Land Commission tract on Coosaw Island, all the residents of the Coosaw Island tract left "the Republican part. [sic] and voted with the Democrat part. [sic] last election."[36] Another settler in Charleston County, Issac B. Rivers, was recognized by Hampton for services "rendered as an active colored Democrat" in the last

33. *News and Courier*, September 13, 1876; Kibler, pp. 486–94.
34. Greenville *Enterprise and Mountaineer*, October 25, 1876.
35. Holland (ed.), p. 254; Tindall, p. 13; Williamson, pp. 409–10.
36. Letter from B. S. Rivers to Wade Hampton, May 23, 1877, Governor Hampton's Papers, S.C.A.

election.[37] Although these instances of "crossing Jordan" are not isolated cases, most converts acted out of fear, not conviction.

The Negroes under the combined pressure of persuasion and intimidation proved to be defenseless. On election day many of them stayed away from the polls. It is no wonder that the Negro majority, spurned by most of the whites and forsaken by both the Republican party and the Federal government, was crushed by a determined opposition bent upon power.

As to the election itself, little need be said; both sides indulged in fraud, both claimed victory, and a dual government existed until April 11, 1877, when the executive office was turned over to Hampton after President Rutherford B. Hayes had virtually decreed it. It was more than leadership, more than simply the methods employed, that had restored the Democrats to power in South Carolina twelve years after the end of the Civil War. President Ulysses S. Grant in a rare moment of insight glimpsed the true significance of the Democratic reaction. "In South Carolina the contest has assumed such a phase that the whole army of the United States would be inadequate to enforce the authority of Governor Chamberlain."[38]

Sheer numerical superiority did not determine the outcome of the election of 1877. The Republicans had the numbers; the Democrats were in the minority, but they possessed a total commitment to the success of a single idea. It was this total commitment to overthrowing the Reconstruction government and restoring home rule that tipped the balance in their favor.

37. Letter from Wade H. Manning (Hampton's private secretary) to W. J. Magrath, June 21, 1878, Wade Hampton Letterbook, Miscellaneous, 1878–1879, p. 263, S.C.A.
38. *The Nation*, XXIV (March 1, 1877).

The gap dividing the Regulars and Reformers proved so great that the two wings of the Republican party could not merge and achieve the necessary solidarity to resist the will of the white opposition. The Democrats, united and subjected to no cross-pressures, generated enough energy to accomplish what appeared on the surface to be impossible. The Negro majority was rolled back, the Reconstruction government was overthrown, and the sovereign power of South Carolina was returned to the white citizenry of the state.

CHAPTER VII

Retrenchment, Efficiency, Economy, and the Land Experiment

THE VIOLENT UPHEAVAL which was expected when the remaining Federal troops were withdrawn from Columbia failed to materialize. Although Reconstruction in South Carolina formally came to an end on that April day in 1877, its legacy lingered.

According to the traditional interpretation, the victors of 1877 immediately and methodically swept away all the equalitarian ideals accumulated in nine years of Republican rule. Supposedly, too, the personnel of the Radical regime were dispersed, the political and social importance of the Negro was reduced to a minimum, and the supremacy of the white race was maintained and justified.[1] This view oversimplifies the situation. South Carolina emerged from Reconstruction with a system of government fluid and flexible, and racial practices between the end of Reconstruction and the 1890's were neither as harsh nor as rigorous as they were to become. Although it would be easy to overemphasize the liberal aspects of this essentially conservative government, opportunities ex-

1. Simkins and Woody, p. 542.

isted for an equitable settlement of the race question, and alternatives were considered before the whites started down the road leading from redemption to full segregation. Extreme racism erupted again in the nineties, accompanied by intimidation, violence, disfranchisement, and Jim Crow laws, but the final betrayal of the Negro did not occur in 1877.[2]

Thirteen years passed before the opportunity for Negroes to obtain land under the Act of 1869 was finally denied them. Not until 1890 was the cycle completed—the land redistribution program was bankrupt and the holdings were reconcentrated in the hands of a few white landowners. To understand the survival of this experiment and certain other Republican institutions in the post-Reconstruction era, the political situation confronting the Redeemers must be considered.

For one thing, the Democratic party in 1877 was not the monolithic structure it had seemed to be during the campaign; it soon became subject to cross pressures and internal dissension. The fundamental differences between the Hampton and the Gary forces, although suppressed during the campaign of 1876, had not been reconciled. While it is true that both Hampton and Gary were loyal South Carolinians who believed in the Confederacy and the need for white solidarity in the Democratic party, important differences in their basic attitudes toward the place of the Negro in South Carolina society made their rivalry continue and become more bitter with the passing of Reconstruction. Hampton and his moderate supporters wished to bind up the wounds inflicted

2. Hampton M. Jarrell, *Wade Hampton and the Negro: The Road Not Taken* (Columbia, 1949); George B. Tindall, *South Carolina Negroes, 1877–1900* (Columbia, 1952); C. Vann Woodward, *Origin of the New South, 1877–1913* (Baton Rouge, 1951); C. Vann Woodward, *The Strange Career of Jim Crow* (New York, 1955); Dewey W. Grantham, Jr., "The Southern Bourbons Revisited," *South Atlantic Quarterly*, LX (Summer, 1961), 286–95; Bernard A. Weisberger, "The Dark and Bloody Ground of Reconstruction Historiography," *The Journal of Southern History*, XXV (November, 1959), 427–47.

by war and Reconstruction and resume normal pursuits without further disrupting society. Although they were conservatives, they were also commercial-minded men seeking to establish an industrialized "New South." The Redeemers, therefore, sought a closer relationship with the North in order to gain a place for their region in the development of business and industry.[3] To placate the North, the Redeemers grasped for a formula that would lead to the assimilation of the Negroes into society without bringing about another resurgence of Negro domination. The Gary forces, on the other hand, eschewed industrialism and sought to advance the agrarian crusade. They turned to the most blatant forms of Negro-baiting to gain popular support, and Gary was the articulate spokesman for the forces of Negrophobia. He pressed for the immediate exclusion of the Negro from the political, economic, and social life of South Carolina.[4] The Hampton moderates, hoping to paper over the cracks in the party, concentrated on those areas in which there was agreement.

All Democrats agreed that the personnel of the Radical regime should be brought to justice. Since something symbolic was needed to fulfill the expectations held by the victorious whites that those manifestly guilty of fraud and corruption during Reconstruction should be tried and convicted, a gigantic legislative investigation was launched to probe the guilt of the deposed Republican officials.[5] As a course of action it certainly was no innovation, since it merely carried forward a

3. Jarrell, pp. 121–50; C. Vann Woodward, *Origins of the New South, passim.* William J. Cooper, Jr., *The Conservative Regime: South Carolina, 1877–1890* (Baltimore: Johns Hopkins Press, 1968) appeared too late for use in this study, but is of great importance for a revisionary estimate of the Redeemer government in South Carolina.

4. Jarrell, pp. 121–50; Francis Butler Simkins, *Pitchfork Ben Tillman* (Baton Rouge: Louisiana State University Press, 1944), pp. 79–80; Tindall, pp. 26–40.

5. Simkins and Woody, p. 542.

movement begun during the Republican administration. Once again the Land Commission was to be investigated.

Representative Samuel Dibble, a lawyer from Orangeburg, headed the special sub-committee reinvestigating the operations of the former Land Commission. Dibble, a staunch opponent of Reconstruction, had been Orangeburg's Democratic county chairman since the Seymour and Grant campaign of 1868 and had been elected to the House in May, 1877.[6] Dibble labored throughout the fall and winter of 1877 gathering testimony against the members of the commission. His findings made clear beyond any doubt that Scott, Neagle, Leslie, Parker, Kimpton, and De Large had been bribe dispensers, bribe gatherers, and embezzlers, guilty of gross fraud while serving as public officials of the Land Commission.[7] His evidence, however, was not published in the *Fraud Report*.[8]

Since the South Carolina legislature in 1877 was overwhelmingly Democratic, it is possible that for appearance's sake a Republican was made chairman of the Investigating Committee to give its findings the aura of impartiality. John R. Cochran, the Republican chosen to be the tool of the Redeemers,

6. Orangeburg *News and Times*, June 2, 1877; Snowden, V, p. 123.
7. In preparing his brief, Dibble collected the necessary evidence to support his charges that the Land Commission administrators were guilty of malfeasance in office (Dibble memoranda, May 9, 1877 [notes to himself on the Land Commission transactions]; Letter from R. J. Donaldson to C. P. Leslie, October 15, 1869; John Neagle to C. P. Leslie, November 17, 1869; Phillip Schley's Land Commission application, February 8, 1870; D. M. Porter to Niles G. Parker, June 6, 1870; D. M. Porter to Daniel Chamberlain, June 6, 1870 (copy); D. M. Porter to Niles G. Parker, June 9, 1870; R. W. Boyd to John R. Cochran, October 23, 1877; MS Affidavit signed by Niles G. Parker, January 23, 1878; MS Affidavit signed by James Simons, Jr., November 1, 1877, Samuel Dibble Papers, Duke University).
8. *Report of the Joint Investigating Committee on Public Frauds and the Election of J. J. Patterson to the United States Senate, Made to the General Assembly at the Regular Session, 1877–1878* (Columbia: State Printers, 1878), cited hereafter as the *Fraud Report, 1877*.

must in turn have used the Democrats in his capacity as chairman to suppress evidence that implicated both him and Scott in the Land Commission frauds. The published *Fraud Report* contained not one word on the Land Commission.

Cochran apparently survived the stigma of having been an active Republican throughout Reconstruction. After his connection with Scott in the Anderson-Pickens-Oconee land swindle had been revealed in the spring of 1870, Cochran did not slink away to the obscurity of his drygoods store in Anderson. Remaining an active Republican in county affairs, he had by mid-summer become chairman of the Anderson County Republican party. At the party's county rally on July 23, 1870, Cochran was recognized as the leading Republican in the county, being elected delegate to the state convention meeting in Columbia on July 29.[9] He rose steadily in the ranks of the party. In 1872 Cochran was elected to serve as a representative from Anderson; two years later he was elected to the state Senate.[10] In 1876 he campaigned in Anderson County as an Independent Republican candidate, and was returned to the Senate.[11] From Cochran's case, it appears that the lines were not so carefully drawn in 1876 as historians once believed, nor were the labels of "carpetbagger" and "scalawag" so positively applied. Cochran is an example of one who emerged in 1877 seemingly unscathed by his political affiliation with the Republican party. Cochran returned to Anderson and his drygoods store after his second term in the Senate ended, and presumably remained until his death a respected member of the community.

In actual fact, the 1,700-page *Fraud Report* brought very

---

9. Anderson *Intelligencer*, June 30, 1870; July 28, 1870; October 13, 1870.

10. *Ibid.*, May 25, 1876. *See also*: Cochran's correspondence in the Governors' Papers, 1868–1876, *passim*, S.C.A.

11. *Senate Journal, 1877–1878*, p. 3; *News and Courier*, November 16, 1876.

little to light that had not already been revealed by Republican investigating committees, but its disclosures were to be interpreted by the Democratic press "as a blanket indictment of all things Republican."[12] It reassured South Carolinians that the Palmetto State had won a moral victory over the North. Moreover, whenever the extremist element of the Republican party "waved the bloody shirt," presumably South Carolina Democrats could remind the Republicans of their misconduct in office by bringing out their leather bound copies of the *Fraud Report*. In addition, indictments under South Carolina law were instituted against those reported to be the worst offenders. These indictments, however, were used more as a lever to put pressure on President Hayes than from a desire to bring the guilty to justice.[13] Since the avowed goals of Hampton's administration were to bind up wounds and resume normal pursuits interrupted by war and Reconstruction, retribution formed no part of his program. He struck a bar-

12. Tindall, pp. 18–19; Williamson, pp. 414–15. That such was the intention of the administration was made evident in a letter written by Attorney General James Conner to Lieutenant Governor William Simpson. Conner wrote that the publication of such a report "would politically guillotine every man of them" (August 24, 1877, William Dunlap Simpson Papers, Duke University).

13. James F. Izlar, a highly respected lawyer in Orangeburg, later to be successively state senator, judge of the First Circuit, and member of Congress, made known his distaste for instituting and conducting trials "in a tribunal of justice for the purpose of accomplishing party objects." Furthermore, he wrote that many Democrats agreed with him and looked upon the trials "with undisguised disapprobation, because they believe that the charges are frivolous or unfounded. . ." (James F. Izlar to W. St. Julien Jervey, Solicitor of the First Circuit, October 10, 1877, S.C.A.).

Fewer than 25 persons were eventually indicted, and of these only L. Cass Carpenter, Francis L. Cardozo, and Robert Smalls were tried, convicted, and sentenced before the Court of General Sessions for Richland County, in November, 1877 (*Reports of Cases Heard and Determined by the Supreme Court of South Carolina*, XI, pp. 195–261, 265–75). Cardozo was convicted of conspiracy as treasurer for cashing certain coupons on state bonds which had been fraudulently obtained by the holders but which were identical to legitimate coupons. He was pardoned within a few months.

gain with Hayes whereby in return for minimizing the state's prosecution of Republican offenders, the President would exercise clemency on behalf of South Carolinians involved in violations of the Ku Klux laws, in the Hamburg and Ellenton riots, and in revenue cases.[14] Formally, the legal entanglements were not all removed until 1884, yet as early as June, 1878, most South Carolinians under Federal indictment could return home with the assurance from Hayes "that no action shall be taken against any of these parties and that should any be brought up it shall be at once *nolle pros'd.*"[15] Although an amnesty agreement had been worked out between Hayes and Hampton, there remained one individual—Kimpton, the New York financial agent—whom the governor was determined to prosecute for his crimes in connection with the Land Commission scandals. After repeated failures to have Kimpton extradited by the Massachusetts governor,[16] Hampton employed a New York private detective, Thomas H. Ross, to get his man. Ross telegraphed him on March 19, 1879: "H. H. Kimpton left the state before I received your second telegram. . . . If you will write me informing me what it is worth to get him, also send me a warrant at the same time, I will arrest him on his return."[17] But Kimpton evidently evaded Ross; nothing more is known of the financial agent.

After Hampton's success in "burying the hatchet" between North and South had freed him from fear of outside intervention, party rivalry between the Hampton moderates and

14. *New York Times*, September 1, 1877; Jarrell, pp. 136–37, 175–86 (reprints correspondence between Hampton and Hayes on the subject); McKitrick, pp. 248–49.

15. Letter of Wade Hampton to Colonel John Bratton, June 14, 1878, Wade Hampton Letterbook, Miscellaneous, 1878–1879, S.C.A.

16. Letter from Governor Alexander H. Rice to Wade Hampton, August 30, 1878, Governor Hampton's Papers.

17. Telegram from Thomas H. Ross to Wade Hampton, March 19, 1879, Telegrams, Governor Hampton's Papers.

the Gary extremists over the status of the Negro seemed to accelerate. Hampton, in advocating a program of conciliation toward the Negro and in attempting to redeem the pledges made during the campaign of 1876, appointed many black men to county offices throughout the state.[18] According to the compilations of the former director of the Archives, the late Dr. J. Harold Easterby, 116 Negroes were appointed to office by Wade Hampton.[19]

The liberal behavior of Hampton toward the Negroes must not be exaggerated. It was largely negative, merely promising to retain the rights gained for the Negro by others. But Hampton's program of white supremacy saw no necessary correlation between white supremacy and Negro proscription.[20] The Gary

18. Wade Hampton Appointments, 1877–1878, *passim*, S.C.A.; Letter from colored petitioners of Cross Anchor to Wade Hampton, June 15, 1877, Loose Papers, Wade Hampton; Letter from Y. J. Pope to Wade Hampton, December 23, 1876; Letter from George B. Tindall to Dr. J. Harold Easterby, November 3, 1951 (copy), S.C.A.

19. County Officers

Office	Negro Appointments
Clerk of Court	2
Coroner	1
County Commissioner	16
Debt Commissioner	3
Elections Commissioner	26
Jury Commissioner	7
Justice Commissioner	28
Notary Commissioner	10
Pilotage	1
Probate Judge	5
School Commissioner	5
Sheriff	1
Steam Commissioner	1
Treasurer	3
Total	109
Other Officers	7
	116

Loose Papers, Governor Hampton's Papers.

20. Tindall, p. 21.

forces, on the other hand, were not so optimistic. They contended that it would be impossible to maintain white control for any length of time in a state that had a black majority with a tendency dating back to Union League days of voting as a bloc. But for the time being, extremism was suppressed, and institutions for the welfare of the Negroes continued during Hampton's administration. Hampton's policy of moderation would work as long as he could convince South Carolinians that it was successful. The election of 1878, in which most of the black constituency voted the Democratic ticket, appeared to sustain Hampton in his belief that mutual benefits could be derived from continuing to permit Negroes to exercise their basic rights. Moreover, for as long as the Redeemers remained convinced that the land experiment could be a financial asset to the state, they would not let it perish.

Retrenchment, efficiency, and economy—these were the key words of the Democratic administration. The Redeemers looked upon the sale of former Land Commission lands as a source of revenue for replenishing the depleted state treasury. Indeed, with this objective in mind, certificates of purchase issued by Cardozo and Hayne were allowed to remain in effect, and new county agents were appointed to collect payments.[21] Moreover, Robert M. Sims, Hampton's secretary of state, set about at once to ascertain how many Land Commission lots were still unsettled.

Sims encountered difficulty from the very start. Since many of Hayne's records of accounts with settlers were missing,[22] the only way Sims could know the disposition of tracts or the progress of settlement was from the certificates of purchase. He had no record, however, of those settlers who had not been

21. *Repts. and Resols., 1877–1878,* p. 353; *Repts. and Resols., 1878,* p. 386.
22. *See* Appendix I.

issued certificates because they had not resided on the tract for three years.[23] In addition, Sims's task was made more complex when heirs of some landowners, who had sold to the Land Commission property in Chesterfield, Laurens, and Pickens counties, sued to repossess these tracts held by the state, claiming that the state's titles were defective and thereby invalid.[24] Sims was at a loss to prove otherwise without involving the state in drawnout litigation. And if this were not enough, reports soon reached Sims of white men who were misrepresenting themselves as the new county agents of the Land Commission appointed by Hampton to collect payments.[25] Cardozo had encountered the same thing during his administration and had acted to remedy the situation by appointing a single agent, J. E. Green. Now Sims, confronted with an identical problem, concluded, "This land business is in a bad mess."[26]

Sims suspected B. F. Bates of Spartanburg, implicated in former Land Commission scandals with De Large, of assuming authority over lands he had no legitimate right to administer and of collecting installments from the unsuspecting Negro settlers. The purchase and rent money collected by Bates never found its way to the office of the secretary of state.[27] Sims was wary of making accusations against Bates, for despite Bates's Republican affiliation during Reconstruction, he was now in good standing with the Democrats. Hampton

23. This probably accounts for Sims's estimate that in 1877, 47,000 acres of former Land Commission lands remained unsold (*Repts. and Resols., 1877–1878*, p. 353). In 1877 the only unsold land was probably 22,000 acres of the Schley plantations in Charleston and Colleton counties.

24. Record of Sinking Fund Book B, pp. 154–55, S.C.A.

25. Two letters from R. M. Sims to H. S. Farley, October 13, 1877, October 16, 1877, Secretary of State, Commission Letters, 1870–1878, S.C.A.

26. Letter from R. M. Sims to Mrs. Allen, July 17, 1877, Secretary of State, Commission Letters, 1870–1878.

27. Sims to Farley, October 16, 1877.

had appointed him trial justice for Spartanburg County as the reward for his services during the campaign of 1876.[28] Sims, therefore, felt he had to be absolutely certain of his ground before accusing Bates. He wrote Captain Hugh Farley, editor of the *Carolina Spartan* in Spartanburg, of his conviction "that he [Bates] has in this line actually sold and rented lands that have never been reported to this office." Sims asked Farley to investigate the matter and get to the bottom of Bates's duplicity.[29] In the meantime he warned Negro settlers in Spartanburg not to pay any money to unauthorized persons, naming Bates in particular as one "not authorized to receive any rents, and you must not pay him any."[30]

The secretary of state, exasperated over the loss of some of the Land Commission records and harassed by such petty annoyances as the Bates business, but lacking the funds to institute an investigation of the entire Land Department on his own initiative, demanded that the legislature draft a comprehensive plan for the disposition of the Land Commission tracts owned by the state.[31] In December, 1877, the legislature complied by passing an act giving the secretary of state the necessary authority and budget "to ascertain . . . what lands have been purchased for the State under the Land Commission and in what counties, the prices paid, whether the State has received titles, and to which and what disposition has been made to said lands."[32]

Sims at once ordered the county auditors to assume the duties of sub-land-commission agents. They were to inform the secretary of state of the status of the lands, the names of all

28. Hampton Appointments, 1877–1878, March 1877, S.C.A.; John H. Ennis to Wade Hampton, December 26, 1876, Governor Hampton's Papers.
29. Sims to Farley, October 16, 1877.
30. Sims to Allen, July 17, 1877.
31. *Repts. and Resols., 1877–1878*, p. 386.
32. *Acts and Joint Resolutions, 1875–1878*, XVI, p. 637.

settlers, and the payment that had been made on the land. Sims told the auditors that by assuming this additional authority they could do their job of collecting taxes more intelligently and properly. As an added incentive, these agents were allowed to keep 10 to 11 per cent of all they collected on prior sales and 5 per cent on new cash sales of lots to settlers.[33]

Not all of Sims's problems, however, were so easily solved. Disputes over the legality of the state's titles to certain lands made for continuing difficulty. In particular, the title to one of the Schley tracts in Colleton—purchased by the Advisory Board to pay off Leslie—was in doubt. Sims summarized what little he knew of this transaction and asked Attorney General LeRoy F. Youmans for an opinion as to who legally possessed the land:

> A tract of land in Colleton County was sold to the state by P. T. Schley for the sum of $19,000 date of conveyance February 21st 1870—date of record in R. M. C. Office Nov. 28th 1871. On April 19th 1870 this land was mortgaged by Schley to B. Riker; on 2nd of May 1870 this mortgage was transferred to P. W. Fairey and on Dec. 4 1871 was sold by the sheriff under foreclosure of mortgage to P. W. Fairey. Observe this mortgage was made [Schley to Riker] 59 days after conveyance to Leslie but before the latter was recorded . . . .[34]

Sims was understandably confused. He asked the attorney general, "Has the State a title to the lands and if so what steps should be taken to repossess it?"[35] The answer was slow in coming. Not until 1889, after lengthy legal proceedings, were all of the Schley lands recovered by the state.[36]

33. Letters from R. M. Sims to N. Gregorie of Yemassee, S. C., January 12, 1878; R. M. Sims to J. T. Robertson of Abbeville, S. C., February 13, 1878, Secretary of State, Commission Letters, 1870–1878.
34. February 11, 1878, Secretary of State, Commission Letters, 1870–1878.
35. *Ibid.*
36. Minutes of the Sinking Fund Commission, November 6, 1883–April 9, 1889, *passim*, S.C.A.

In addition to encountering organizational defects and legal entanglements, Sims clashed from the very beginning with those who would continue the program unchanged. Since Land Commission sales were supposed to be a revenue-making venture for the Democrats committed to economy, it seemed unreasonable to the secretary of state for anyone to pretend that it was a humanitarian enterprise. Sims wanted to oust persons immediately who were failing to meet their annual payments, and as a more efficient means of redistributing these forfeited lands, "to sell the tracts in bulk for no less than it cost the State . . . to sell the whole tract in lump or to parties."[37] When the Advisory Board refused to go along with him, Sims went to the legislature and demanded they take some action. Moreover, in addition to eviction of delinquent settlers and bulk sale of their forfeited land, he advocated new terms of purchase requiring that new settlers make full payment within three or four years instead of the current eight-year contract.[38] This last point the legislature agreed to. Certificates of purchase issued prior to 1878 continued in force for eight years, whereas those issued after 1878 called for payment within two to four years. In most instances, the general terms were one-fourth cash, balance in three equal annual installments, with interest at 7 per cent from date of purchase.[39]

The year 1878 had seen other changes in the administration of the Land Commission experiment. These modifications showed how an institution set in motion by the Republicans for the benefit of South Carolina's Negroes, although retained

37. Letter from R. M. Sims to John Watson, August 7, 1877, Secretary of State, Commission Letters. On the same date Sims expressed the same sentiment to a party interested in purchasing a Land Commission tract (Letter from R. M. Sims to N. Walker, August 7, 1877); *Repts. and Resols., 1878*, p. 386.

38. *Repts. and Resols., 1877–1878*, p. 354.

39. Minutes of the Board of Commissioners, 1879–1883, p. 84, S.C.A.; Minutes of the Sinking Fund Commission, November 6, 1883–April 9, 1889, p. 273.

by the Democrats, was reshaped and remolded to meet their needs. By the act of March 22, 1878, the former Land Commission lands still held by the secretary of state became subject to the direction and instructions of the commissioners of the Sinking Fund.[40] By this same act the Advisory Board's resolution of April 1, 1872—to sell land to settlers at the market price —was struck down. Thereafter, the lots were to be sold at the price paid by the state.[41] Through the passage of this act, and its subsequent amendment of December 24, 1878,[42] Sims had scored his point. The Redeemers' land experiment policy was becoming more rigid; it was being retained to help extinguish the public debt.

The Sinking Fund Commission is another example of an institution created by the Republicans and retained by the Democrats. The original reason for the establishment, in March, 1870, of the Sinking Fund Commission was to enable the "railroad ring"—Scott, Chamberlain, Neagle, Parker, Leslie, Kimpton, *et al.*, to secure from the state at nominal prices stock in the Greenville and Columbia Railroad. To this end the act was passed, authorizing the newly created commission to sell all unproductive state property. It was consummated by the sale of 21,698 shares of stock in the Greenville and Columbia Railroad Company (which had cost the state $20 per share, aggregating $433,960) at $2.75 per share, aggregating $59,669.50. The stock was sold without advertisement on the day after the bill passed, and was paid for by Kimpton's receipt as the financial agent in New York. "No money passed and the

40. *Acts and Joint Resolutions, 1875–1878*, XVI, pp. 558–59.
41. *Ibid.*, p. 559.
42. *Ibid.*, p. 811. Sims requested the amendment, repealing all acts inconsistent with this act, because the act of March 22, 1878, "leaves great doubts as to how much of the old acts are repealed and how much are in force, and actually what laws and rules are to govern the Land Commissioner now in the performance of his duties" (*Repts. and Resols., 1877–1878*, p. 386).

funds transferred to Kimpton's books were sunk beyond recovery in the devious processes of hypothecation and general
bond swindling. . . ."[43]

Throughout Reconstruction the Sinking Fund Commission
was subject to many investigations, but—as with those of the
Land Commission—the guilty went unpunished. Nevertheless,
by the act of March 22, 1878, the legislature restored to the
Sinking Fund Commission its legal function of receiving in-
come and revenues of the state and paying off the state's current indebtedness. The formal structure remained the same,
and to the commission—consisting of the governor, comptroller general, attorney general, chairman of the Senate Finance Committee, and chairman of the House Ways and
Means Committee—was delegated the authority to sell state-
owned land. It was given broad power, and sales were to be
made in such a manner as the commissioners deemed most ad-
vantageous to the state.[44] Under the direction of the Sinking
Fund commissioners, Negroes who defaulted in their payments on certificates of purchase were to be evicted and their
lands resold.[45] The Redeemers undoubtedly supposed their
changes in policy would set right an altogether deplorable
situation inherited from their Radical predecessors.

Under the new terms of sale, fewer Negroes took up certificates of purchase, and many already settled on the tracts were
evicted, their lands forfeited because of the stricter application

43. Report of the Joint Committee to investigate the transactions of the
Sinking Fund Commission, *Repts. and Resols., 1872–1873*, pp. 753–78. See also
Fraud Report, 1877, pp. 546, 849–50.

44. The Sinking Fund Commission is still functioning but under a new
name. In 1950 the authority of the S.F.C. was delegated to a Budget and Control Board; the composition remained the same (*Code of South Carolina*,
pars. 1–358).

45. *Repts. and Resols., 1879–1880*, p. 422; R. M. Sims to S. S. Tompkins,
January 20, 1879, Land Commission Letterbook #1, January 4, 1879–August 2,
1881, S.C.A.

of collection schedules. For instance, 14 families on the Gooch tract in Marlboro County were evicted at one time, the land forfeited to the state amounting to 657 acres.[46] Before 1878, these 657 acres would have been resold to 14 new applicants, but on this occasion the commissioners accepted the offer of a white man, J. D. Murchison, to purchase the lots in bulk at $8.00 per acre, for a total sum of $5,256.[47]

Not all the settlers gave up the land without a struggle. On the Cross Roads tract in Williamsburg County 25 defaulting families resisted all attempts of the local land agent to evict them. The agent relented and agreed to allow them to remain on as renters for the coming year. Only a few accepted the compromise, the rest selected a spokesman who made clear to the agent their refusal "to come to any terms whatever . . . ." More than four months passed before the sheriff and his deputies succeeded in forcibly removing the settlers.[48]

The census of 1880 showed that a pell-mell rout of Negro settlers had been set off by the Democrats' stricter observance of the laws governing the Land Commission experiment. Generally speaking, there was wholesale abandonment of the least fertile tracts. In regions of poor soil and rugged terrain, settlers, no matter how eager they were to become independent farmers, could not make payments on time and eviction was inevitable. On the more desirable tracts, about half of the original settlers were still in residence in 1880.[49] On the other hand, despite the inflexible application of the new laws with their emphasis on revenue, Negroes had not been entirely deprived of the opportunity to *own* land. Indeed, in practice, the

46. *Repts. and Resols., 1879–1880*, p. 8.
47. *Ibid.*, pp. 8–9.
48. Letter of R. M. Sims to Sinking Fund Commissioners, July 19, 1879, Drawer 51, Division of General Services, S.C. Record Center; *Repts. and Resols, 1879–1880*, p. 422.
49. *See* Appendix II.

Redeemers' policy encouraged ownership. Whereas the Republicans had emphasized actual settlement, it might be said that the Democrats, by insisting on final cash payments and threatening eviction, motivated settlers to gain free and clear title.[50] Moreover, through litigation the Redeemers gained clear title to approximately 6,000 acres of disputed lands in Laurens, Chesterfield, and Aiken counties,[51] thereby augmenting the number of acres available for settlement. With the settlement of this litigation the land purchased by the Land Commission amounted to 118,436 acres.

Although the conciliatory racial policy of the moderates appeared to be weakening even before Hampton's election to the Senate, the new policies were still not absolutely rigid in regard to the settlers. When in January, 1878, the question arose as to whether a further extension of time should be granted on delinquent Land Commission accounts,[52] the legislature chose a lenient policy over one of expediency. The secretary of state was directed to extend for one year (until January, 1879) the deadline for payment due on Land Commission lands.[53]

The final abandonment of the Land Commission experiment came in the decade of the 1880's, at a time when Negroes were being excluded from politics, and when the Redeemers themselves were being rudely displaced.

50. *Repts. and Resols., 1880–1881*, p. 826.
51. Sinking Fund Minute Book "B," December 8, 1882–June 3, 1884 (Secretary of State's copy), pp. 154–55, S.C.A.
52. *Repts. and Resols., 1877–1878*, p. 353.
53. *Acts and Joint Resolutions, 1875–1878*, XVI, p. 644. It should not be overlooked that the one-year extension was probably not only motivated by benevolence—waiting until after crops had been harvested—but also it was politically astute to wait until after the election of 1878.

CHAPTER VIII

The Lost Decade

BETWEEN WADE HAMPTON'S election as governor in 1876 and his departure for the United States Senate in February, 1879, the status of the Negro in South Carolina was undefined. If South Carolina had chosen to follow Gary in 1876 instead of Hampton, the consequences would have been far worse. Gary's supporters ranted on about complete elimination of the Negro from public life, but most prominent South Carolinians went along with Hampton in supporting the Negro in the basic rights guaranteed by the Thirteenth, Fourteenth, and Fifteenth Amendments. The moderates' position seemed justified in 1878, when Hampton won re-election by the overwhelming margin of 119,550 to 213.[1] The Democratic party's fear that a Negro majority would challenge a state government controlled by whites appeared to have been laid to rest. Both races, it seemed, could continue to work together for mutual benefit.[2] The era of cooperation, however, was short-lived. In December, Hampton was elected to the United States Senate, and

---

1. *Repts. and Resols., 1878*, p. 436.
2. Jarrell, pp. 122–143; Tindall, pp. 19–29. *See* survey by staff of South Carolina Archives indicating that 116 Negroes were appointed to county offices by Wade Hampton (Chapter VII, n.19, above).

with his removal from state politics confidence among the moderates disintegrated rapidly.[3]

The moderates were faced again with the old dilemma of how to prevent the Negroes from gaining political ascendancy in the state without restricting their participation in government. They were hard-pressed to find another leader of such personal magnetism as Hampton to attract Negro support for the Democratic party.[4] Looking back, one wonders how long even Hampton could have kept the racial question submerged without having to make concessions to the race-hating extremists. None of those somber men of the 1880's, whose faces stare out at us from their less than flattering photographs, had Hampton's personal attractiveness. Nevertheless, it was left to them to carry out the pledges Hampton left behind when he moved on to the national scene. Hampton's successors neither grasped nor admitted that there were alternatives to the doctrine of uncompromising white supremacy. The Redeemers, fearing a political defeat unless they made concessions to the exponents of race-hating orthodoxy, decided to cooperate with them. Thus began the lost decade in South Carolina politics.

From the governorship of Hagood to that of Richardson, Hampton's influence was not completely removed.[5] Johnson Hagood, elected governor in 1880, pledged equal rights and protection for all, knowing "neither white man nor colored

3. *Senate Journal, 1878*, pp. 112–13. Even before the election of 1878, Johnson Hagood in a letter to former Attorney General James Conner expressed his concern over finding a worthy successor to Hampton. Hagood, believing that Hampton would be elected to the Senate, wrote that Lieutenant Governor "Simpson is going to worry us. He will serve if nominated—a sort of milk and cider position that will hardly do when you have to encounter such people as we have to contend with" (Hagood to Conner, April 27, n.d. [but it must have been 1878], James Conner Papers, South Carolina Historical Society).

4. Jarrell, pp. 158–59; Tindall, pp. 37–38.

5. Tindall, p. 38.

man, but only citizens of South Carolina, alike amenable to her laws and entitled to their protection."[6] Nevertheless, he followed a policy toward the Negro that was something of a compromise between the philosophies of Hampton and Gary. Many of the civil rights gained by the Negroes during Reconstruction were preserved, but the political influence of the Negroes was sharply reduced. Hampton's pledge of a "full vote" was abrogated by the complex "eight box law," enacted by the legislature in 1882,[7] which provided for separate boxes for eight different classes of office. Ostensibly the intent of the "eight box law" was to provide an effective literacy test. The voter was required to choose, by the label, the proper box for his ballot. "In practice, however, it would be simple for election managers to help those illiterates who would vote 'right' and let others void their ballots through ignorance."[8] The Redeemers, thus having disfranchised the majority of Negroes while enfranchising illiterate whites, were soon to be destroyed by the latter.

The Redeemers' policy of appeasement in the 1880's won them neither increased popular confidence nor enhanced political prestige. Although Gary died in 1881, and the "eight box law" of 1882 ended the threat of a Negro voting majority, popular discontent continued to spread. Support for the administration dwindled as state officials proved unable to cope with the continued agricultural distress, refused to give the people an effective voice in the choice of governors, and above all, appeared powerless to arrive at a solution to the Negro problem which was satisfactory to either race.[9] The compromise effected by the moderates became more difficult to main-

6. *House Journal, 1880*, p. 112.
7. *Statutes at Large*, XVII, pp. 1116–21; Jarrell, pp. 158–59.
8. Tindall, p. 69.
9. Simkins, p. 82; Wallace, III, pp. 336–37, 345–50.

tain as more and more South Carolinians came to share the racial phobias which would lead to proscription, segregation, and total disfranchisement.

The conflict between the moderates and extremists played out against the background of the 1880's had tragic consequences for the state. When the weakness of Hampton's policy of conciliation of the Negroes became apparent, principles were sacrificed for a compromise satisfactory to none. (Hampton's success with this policy, opposed by the majority of whites, had hinged on the power of his own immense prestige to persuade the whites to uphold it, as well as the power of his personal magnetism to attract and hold black voters.) Perhaps further concessions need not have been made. For instance, in regard to the Land Commission experiment, the Redeemers might have undertaken large-scale redistribution of the land. This might in turn have gained them the continued support of the large landowners in need of the capital that sales to the state would have given them. Moreover, it might have won over tenant farmers and sharecroppers of both races by ameliorating their economic distress. If the tracts had been segregated, the whites probably would have participated, and and the passions of the period might have been allayed.

During the remaining years of Redeemer rule the imperfect solution disintegrated rapidly. The clamor for the abandonment of the Negro intensified, and instead of scrapping the compromise and seeking a clearcut commitment to inter-racial goodwill, the Redeemers eventually wearied of the struggle and capitulated. The final impetus for the overthrow of the Redeemers came with the rise of Benjamin R. Tillman, the energetic successor to Martin W. Gary. He captured the Democratic party by a movement that was in part a mixture of agrarian discontent and Negrophobia which had been brewing since the 1870's.[10] Hampton and his followers opposed Tillman in 1890 as they had Gary in 1880,[11] but this time the outcome was different. The Redeemers' policy of appeasement had miscarried. The increasing restrictions of Negro rights neither buttressed their position nor forestalled their overthrow, and in 1890 they lost control of the party to Tillman and his "wool-hats."[12]

Important as was the story of disfranchisement in the 1880's, it was not the only devastating blow dealt the Negro. Negro landownership sponsored and supported by the state was unpopular with the majority of whites who sought a ready, ample, and dependent labor supply.[13] Nevertheless, during Governor Hagood's administration (1880–1882) the right of Negroes to purchase state lands at nominal cost was sustained. In fact, Negro settlement, languishing since 1878, was resuscitated in 1881 by a revision in the Sinking Fund Commission's policy reducing the price of state land to its market value. For instance, the price of the Geiger tract in Lexington County, containing more sand hills than fertile soil, was reduced from $4.00 to $1.35 an acre.[14] The commissioners, recognizing the impossibility of selling the Schley lands—Wythewood and

10. *See* "The Shell Manifesto," *News and Courier*, January 23, 1890; Tindall, p. 73; Wallace, III, pp. 345–50.

11. Johnson Hagood was supported for governor in the Democratic convention of 1880 against Martin W. Gary by Hampton, who reportedly threatened to resign his Senate seat and run against Gary if the latter were nominated (William Arthur Sheppard, *Red Shirts Remembered* [Atlanta: Ruralist Press, 1940], p. 279). In 1890 the Redeemers bolted the convention and nominated Colonel A. C. Haskell for governor (Wallace, III, p. 349).

12. Tillman received 59,159 votes to Haskell's 14,828 (*Repts. and Resols., 1890*, I, p. 604).

13. For an excellent summary of Negroes in agriculture in South Carolina, 1877–1900, *see* Tindall, pp. 92–123. *See also*: State Board of Agriculture of South Carolina, *South Carolina: Resources and Population, Institutions and Industries* (Charleston: Walker, Evans and Cogswell, 1883), *passim*.

14. Minutes of Sinking Fund Commission, 1879–1883, p. 193.

Awendaw—even to the most ignorant Negro at the price paid by the Advisory Board, reduced these properties to $1.00 an acre. At that price, even "Hell Hole Swamp" was partially disposed of to the black settlers. Jack and George Manigault, probably former slaves on the Awendaw place, were among the first to acquire part of it at these low prices. Each man bought 111 acres[15] and cultivated for themselves as free men land on which they had once toiled as slaves. Moreover, by allowing the settlers to reside on the more inferior tracts in Charleston, Colleton, and Georgetown counties for one year free of charge, this land was cleared, improved, and subsequently sold.[16]

Despite increasing Negro settlement and purchase, 57,761 acres of former Land Commission tracts were still in the hands of the state in 1884,[17] an increase of 35,603 acres over the amount unsold in 1877. Although the Sinking Fund Commission's recovery of some hithertofore disputed tracts accounted for some of the increase, the rapid settlement of tracts in the beginning of the decade should have decreased the commission's holdings appreciably. In actual fact, however, more Negroes were losing their lots than were purchasing them. The commissioners, in their zeal to convert the vacant Land Commission tracts into assets providing revenue and taxes for the state, had revised price schedules to make purchasing seem overwhelmingly desirable, but they had not correspondingly readjusted the terms of purchase; settlers were still obligated to pay for the land within three years of the date of purchase. Many settlers, responding to the promise of independence

15. *Ibid.*, pp. 204–206; Sinking Fund Minutes Book "B," December 8, 1882–June 3, 1884, p. 157.

16. *Repts. and Resols., 1881–1882*, p. 1463. For implementation of this policy in other sections of the state, *see* Sinking Fund Commission Letterbook #2, March 1, 1881–August 12, 1882, *passim*, S.C.A.

17. Minutes of Sinking Fund Commission, November 6, 1883–April 9, 1889, p. 77.

through the purchase of cheap land, found themselves caught in the grip of an agricultural depression, and the administrators of the Sinking Fund, unmindful of their plight, proceeded to enforce rigorously the forfeiture laws.[18] The desired result—forcing recalcitrant Negro settlers magically to bring forth overdue payments on certificates of purchase—did not occur. The harsh action of the commissioners, in fact, had just the opposite effect, and the number of acres to be resold increased. Settlers on the poorest, least productive tracts pleaded for an extension of time, but to no avail;[19] consequently they either abandoned the land voluntarily or waited to be evicted from their homesteads. The lands thus forfeited to the state were the least productive and therefore the most difficult to sell; after the mid-1880's, few Negroes could be persuaded to take up homesteads on the poorer tracts.[20]

"A time to plant" gave way to "a time to pluck up that which is planted." The commissioners, feeling in no way responsible for the plight of the Negroes, at this juncture withdrew even their limited commitment to making them landowners.

As early as 1878 Sims had proposed selling whole tracts or large portions thereof as the most expedient way to dispose of the state's holdings. But for a few years his persuasive argument had been resisted by what remained of the Redeemers' sense of obligation to the freedmen. There were, of course, some exceptions. The Gooch transaction has already been

18. *Acts and Joint Resols., 1882–1884*, p. 398; *Acts and Joint Resols., 1885–1887*, pp. 87, 862–66.
19. The records are filled with Land Commission lots forfeited to the state for non-payment on certificates of purchase (Direct Index; Tax Titles A; Tax Titles B; Abstract of Discharge of Forfeited Lands, 1881–1893; Forfeited Land Reports, Returns of Land Commission Agents, S.C.A. *See also* Letters of county auditors to Secretary of State R. M. Sims, Drawer 51, *passim*, Division of General Services, S. C. Record Center).
20. Forfeited Land Reports, Returns of Land Commission Agents, *passim*.

cited, and in December, 1880, a large portion—678 acres—of the Burns tract in Edgefield County was sold to one buyer, A. J. Norris, and all of the Bigger tract—615 acres—had been sold to Peter Dukes.[21] Nevertheless, the policy of selling small individual lots had prevailed for the time being. The repudiation of the Negro as a landowner by the Sinking Fund Commission was marked by no official statement, no evidence more apparent than the increasing propensity of the commissioners after 1883 to consolidate the lots forfeited to the state and to offer them for sale in bulk. At the August 1, 1883, meeting of the Sinking Fund Commission, the secretary of state, James Lipscomb, submitted John Remfrey's application to purchase the unsold portion of Awendaw, which was 10,909 acres, and the unsold Wythewood tract of 6,100 acres. Remfrey offered $10,000[22] for 17,009 acres that had cost the state $60,000, yet the application was endorsed. No voice protested the abandonment of a principle. As has been noted earlier, the majority of Negroes were disenfranchised as early as 1882. Only one year had elapsed before Negro participation in the redistribution of former Land Commission lands was severely restricted. The endorsement of Remfrey's application to purchase 17,009 acres[23] marks the moment that the Sinking Fund Commission virtually overturned the Land Commission Act of 1869 in favor of expediency. This reversal of policy struck at the very

21. Sinking Fund Commission Minutes, 1879–1883, pp. 48, 57. Two other exceptions were the acceptance at the July 6, 1880, meeting of a bid from L. B. Padgett to purchase 251¼ acres of Rice Hope tract and the acceptance at the July 6, 1882, meeting of an offer of R. C. Reeves to purchase 240½ acres of the Harrison tract (*Ibid.*, pp. 46, 178–79).

22. Sinking Fund Minutes Book B, December 8, 1882–June 3, 1884, pp. 139–40.

23. Remfrey reneged on the sale. Scattered throughout the minutes of the Sinking Fund Commission (Minutes, November 6, 1883–April 9, 1889) are references to his "intended purchase," but there is neither a record of sale nor a deed issued to John Remfrey.

core of the experiment; a small homesteader obviously could not compete in sales of such magnitude.

Having once been tried and judged a success, the altered policy was carried through to its logical conclusion. After 1883, although both methods of sale—in bulk or by single lots—were conducted simultaneously, the selling of whole tracts became the preferred method.[24] The Redeemers had apparently capitulated to the demands of race-hating orthodoxy in economics as well as in politics. By 1887 only 26,158 acres of former Land Commission land remained to be sold.[25] Of this balance, 15,691 acres were conveyed by 10 deeds issued in 1888—an average of 1,500 acres each.[26]

Twenty years after the Reconstruction legislature had enacted land reform legislation, superimposing the National Homestead Act upon a single state, and specifying that no less than 25 acres nor more than 100 acres be sold to actual settlers, the cycle was almost completed. Neither the enactment of new legislation nor the abolishment of the old, not even a political announcement heralded the final disintegration of the experiment. It was done simply by deed. For instance, on Lincoln's birthday, 1889, the Sinking Fund Commission conveyed to T. D. Johnstone 1,910¾ acres of the Mary Gilbert Tract in Colleton County.[27] In October deeds were issued conveying almost 1,900 acres to Samuel G. Stoney.

The Stoney family before the war had been part of the planter aristocracy of the low country, but war and Reconstruction had reduced the family's holdings, as they had many

24. Minutes of Sinking Fund Commission, Novmber 6, 1883—April 9, 1889, *passim.*

25. *Ibid.,* p. 293; Duplicate titles B, 1881–1887; *Repts. and Resols., 1886,* pp. 359, 370–71.

26. Minutes of Sinking Fund Commission, 1883–1889, p. 383; Duplicate titles C, State of South Carolina, pp. 3–12.

27. Minutes of Sinking Fund Commission, 1883–1889, p. 411; Duplicate titles C, State of South Carolina, p. 19.

others of their social class. James J. Stoney summed up the general condition of the family in his application for appointment as trial justice: "I am stationary and not likely ever to get away from here with a family to support and very little left to support them on, if there is the smallest pecuniary advantage in holding the office [trial justice], I claim preferment over all others in this Township . . . ."[28] Nevertheless, it appears that during the 1880's some members of the Stoney family began prospering again. On October 30, 1889, the Sinking Fund Commission conveyed deeds to Samuel G. Stoney for two former Land Commission tracts in Charleston County—Blue House and Ararat—aggregating a total of 1,861.88 acres.[29] Thus the story ended as it had begun in 1860 with the restoration of the plantations;[30] by 1890 much of the land commission holdings were concentrated in the hands of a few white families. Of the 118,436 acres purchased by the Land Commission, 68,355 acres had been conveyed to whites, whereas the Negroes owned only 44,579 acres. Fifty-five hundred acres remained unsold.[31]

Moreover, the Negroes learned that in South Carolina political, social, and economic freedom, relatively undefined in 1877, had evolved into a system of caste based upon race, even

28. Letter from James J. Stoney to L. F. Youmans, January 29, 1877, Loose Papers, Governor Hampton's Papers.

29. Duplicate titles C, State of South Carolina, p. 28; Minutes of Sinking Fund Commission, 1883–1889, p. 356.

30. Many of the large plantations in 1890 were not owned by the same families who held them at the end of the war. Immediately after the war the newspapers were filled with advertisements of plantations for sale. Many were purchased by northerners and in turn were resold by them to other people during the 1870's and 1880's.

31. The total number of acres conveyed to Negroes and whites has been determined from the following: Office Secretary of State, Duplicate Titles A, 1872–1880; Duplicate Titles B, 1881–1887; Duplicate Titles C, 1887–1924. The last known parcel of land, containing 825 acres, was conveyed to Julius P. Icord on September 26, 1924 (Duplicate Titles C).

before the political annihilation of the Redeemers. In his inaugural address in 1888, John P. Richardson, the last of the Redeemer governors, echoed all of the sentiments of Negrophobia that had been cultivated by uncompromising white supremacists since the 1870's:

> But to one unalterable purpose we should unfalteringly adhere, and keep its imperative necessity ever present before us, for it is as strong in its obligations as the law of self-preservation. Whatever the future may have in store for us, whether of peaceful development or of exciting agitation, the eternal laws of God in the impress of inferiority they have ineffaceably stamped upon one race, have decreed, the true interest of humanity demands, the sacred memories of the past enjoin, the holy duty we owe to posterity irresistably impels, that we declare with a determination as fixed and immovable as the stars of heaven, that never again shall any other than Anglo-Saxon supremacy rule the destiny of this fair, beloved and beautiful South land of ours.[32]

During the decade of the 1880's the Negro had been all but excluded from the political, economic, and social life of the state. Many of the Land Commission settlers had been deprived of their small farms and forced into share-cropping, with its concomitant evils of inequality, submission, and segregation.

32. *House Journal, 1888*, p. 138.

EPILOGUE

Promised Land

THE SOUTH CAROLINA Land Commission's experiment in two decades of existence had failed to be assimilated into the culture. By 1890 the conservative form of wealth—large landholdings—and with it the one-crop system of agriculture had been restored. Yet something positive remained. Although most of the Land Commission settlers were deprived of their lands, some retained their holdings and achieved relative economic freedom within the state. At least 960 Land Commission deeds had been conveyed before October, 1889.[1] A few Negroes who purchased lots in the 1870's were even able to increase their holdings in the 1880's.[2] The majority of those

1. Land Commission deed books are missing for the period before December 23, 1872, and between March, 1880, and February, 1881. According to the records that are available, 960 deeds had been conveyed to Negroes by 1890 (Office of Secretary of State, Duplicate Titles A, 1872–1880; Duplicate Titles B, 1881–1887; Duplicate Titles C, 1887–1924, State of South Carolina; *Repts. and Resols., 1872–1873*, pp. 154–223). Unfortunately for this study, census records on agriculture did not classify farm owners according to race until 1900, but in 1900 South Carolina Negroes owned 15,503 farms (Tindall, p. 121, citing Bureau of the Census, *Negroes in the United States*, pp. 310–311).
2. Twenty families are known to have increased their holdings to well over 100 acres of Land Commission lands. Probably many more Negroes increased their holdings during the post-Reconstruction era, purchasing the land from

who received Land Commission deeds did not buy more than the original tract, but they managed to hold on tenaciously to what they had.

What were the effects of landownership upon these Negroes? To what extent and under what conditions did the State of South Carolina benefit from this Reconstruction experiment? The subsequent history of these landowners is difficult to trace. The struggle of these settlers to keep their lands in the face of white hostility, the refusal to let go of the land even though unprofitable, the endeavors to scrape together enough tax money each year to retain the land, the economic readjustment to modern agriculture, the prosperity of a few despite these handicaps—none of this apparently has been recorded by those who have experienced these struggles. Inasmuch as three generations have been reared since the original settlers acquired their land from the Land Commission, and their heirs in many instances must have sold off or lost possession of the lots, it seemed unlikely that at this late date we could find a tract still held together in a unit by descendants of the original owners. Fortunately, however, such was not the case.

During Leslie's administration three contiguous tracts were purchased by the Land Commission from the Samuel Marshall family in Abbeville. Samuel Marshall's son, Joseph Warren Waldo Marshall, a physician, apparently was more interested in speculating in land than in practicing medicine. In 1845 he began making extensive land purchases around the county, buying up land warrants from veterans of the Revolutionary War and the War of 1812 and adding them to the family's holdings. On the death of Samuel Marshall, the family at-

---

their less capable neighbors, but only 20 families went through the procedure of purchasing directly from the state (Office of Secretary of State, Duplicate Titles A, 1872–1880; Duplicate Titles B, 1881–1887; Duplicate Titles C, 1887–1924, State of South Carolina).

tempted to sell part of this inheritance to the Land Commission.[3]

None other than James L. Orr, a son-in-law of Samuel Marshall[4]—at that time a circuit judge and a Republican—was chosen by the family to act in their behalf in effecting the sale of their land to the Land Commission. Orr wrote Governor Scott offering to sell the three tracts of land, totaling 2,742 acres, for $10 an acre.[5] Scott brought Orr's application to the attention of the Advisory Board, which authorized Leslie to negotiate the sale at $25,000. Orr declined Leslie's offer, insisting that the lands be purchased for no less than $27,420. Since neither party could agree on a compromise, negotiations between Orr and the land commissioner were terminated, and in October, 1869, the Advisory Board instructed Leslie to wait until other lands were offered for sale from Abbeville.[6]

Within the month the local Land Commission agent in Abbeville County wrote urging Scott to buy the Marshall lands, because the Democrats were planning to form a company to buy them. "They are making arrangements to give one dollar more per acre than we can possible [sic] give and are also trying to prevent us from buying any land whatever in this county. If the land is not bought the party is lost in this district...."[7] The governor acted quickly and the state bought the three Marshall tracts in November and December, 1869, and January, 1870, for Orr's original asking price of $10 an acre, or a total of $27,420.[8] The smallest tract, described as

3. Sketch of Joseph Warren Waldo Marshall; Letter from G. W. Marshall to John H. Marshall, October 21, 1872, Joseph W.W. Marshall Collection, Duke University.

4. James L. Orr to his wife, January 12, 1872, Orr-Patterson Papers, Southern Historical Collection; Anderson *Intelligencer*, March 27, 1873.

5. James L. Orr to Robert K. Scott, October 17, 1869, Governor Scott's Papers.

6. Minutes of the Advisory Board, October 21, 1869.

7. J. Hollinshead to Scott, November 3, 1869, Governor Scott's Papers.

8. Purchase Book, Land Commissioner's Office.

good land and containing 440 acres, was divided into eight plots and sold immediately at $10 an acre to Negro settlers.[9] The remaining two tracts, described as poor worn-out fields broken up by washes and gullies,[10] were less easily disposed of. Only six lots were sold in the first year. After the price had been reduced in 1872 from $10 to the more just price of $6 an acre, and in some cases even lower, all but two lots were taken up.[11] By March, 1884, the settlers had completed their purchases; 49 deeds had been issued.[12]

At a marker dedication ceremony in October, 1963, I met a descendant of the Marshall family of Abbeville, Mrs. Marshall Mays, the former Jane Brooks Marshall. She told me about the old Marshall tract just a few miles from Greenwood. During Reconstruction this tract had been renamed "Promised Land" by the Negro settlers. Many descendants of those settlers were still in residence.[13] Mrs. Mays invited me to visit Promised Land at my earliest convenience.[14]

Armed with a photostat of the original Marshall-tract map, drawn in 1870 by the Land Commission surveyor, and carrying Cardozo's report, which listed most of the names of the original Land Commission settlers, Wylma Wates, reference archivist of the South Carolina Department of Archives and History, and I drove the 80 miles from Columbia to Greenwood to meet Mrs. Marshall Mays and her father-in-law, the late Calhoun Mays, Sr., who were to guide us through the com-

9. Account of Sales A, Secretary of State's Office.
10. *Repts. and Resols., 1872–1873*, p. 142.
11. Account of Sales A, Secretary of State's Office; *Repts. and Resols., 1872–1873*, pp. 142, 155–56.
12. Office of Secretary of State, Duplicate Titles A, 1872–1880; Duplicate Titles B, 1881–1887.
13. In the meantime the Rushland tract on John's Island has been found to contain many descendants of the original owners (Mrs. R. F. Cole to Francis M. Hutson, August 2, 1965, S.C.A.).
14. Interview with Mrs. Marshall Mays, October 9, 1963.

munity. Together we drove the remaining few miles to Promised Land. It would have helped had we been experts in field
work, able to analyze the effect on the Negroes of landownership over a long period of time, the forces operating within
the community that may have made these Negroes different
from rural Negroes in general, and the significance, if any, of
the experiment for the state. Nevertheless, we had several fac-
tors operating in our favor. We all had an interest in Southern
history in general and South Carolina history in particular, an
awareness of the race problem, and yet enough detachment,
we hoped, to grasp the significance of what we were to observe.

Surveyor B. F. Jackson had done his work well in preparing
the plat of the Marshall tract; although his map was made in
1870, it directed us through the settlement and helped us locate the original homesteads. A Baptist church, a school, and a
crossroads store were situated in the very places designated on
the plat as the proposed sites for these buildings. As for the
externals of Promised Land, the public school had been built
within the past two years; it is a modern, one-story, well-
lighted brick building centrally located to serve the rural community. It appeared to have good equipment, comfortable
seating arrangements, and a large playground; the Promised
Land school was typical of rural schools being built all over
the state. The church, too, was just another country church—
a small white frame structure—except that this building had
been recently painted. Even the crossroads store was neither
more nor less dilapidated than most general stores in agricultural regions. The dwellings in Promised Land, however, *were*
different. The houses, all of frame, set on rock foundations,
were usually whitewashed with the doors and shutters painted
either blue, red, or green. The average dwelling consisted of
four rooms, with a brick chimney and glass windows, and in
addition most of the homes had screens in the windows. Prom-

ised Land inhabitants were better housed than most rural
Negroes. Usually there was a well in the yard and a cookstove
in the kitchen. Modest gardens, rows of potted plants on the
porches, television antennas, and rail fences gave evidence of
relative prosperity. Practically every farm had a cow and some
calves, pigs, and poultry. The raising and selling of quail and
turkeys had become a source of considerable revenue with
which the residents paid annual taxes. Moreover, some owners
sold homemade blackberry wine—"great for soaking fruit-
cakes," we were informed—to meet their yearly tax assess-
ments.

The fields adjacent to the neat houses and modest gardens,
on the other hand, looked neither fertile nor well cared for.
Mr. Mays, a lawyer in Greenwood, explained the reason for
their apparent poor condition. Few of the Promised Land
owners left wills, hence inheritance is equal. Most estates,
however, are held as units and operated by one or two of the
heirs, usually grandchildren or great-grandchildren of the
original owners, but, since ownership is scattered widely
among all the heirs, there is little incentive to spend money to
improve the land. Moreover, such widely scattered ownership
has led to confused titles, thus the farmer operating the home
place cannot borrow money or mortgage the property to make
improvements. In general, the land is used only to grow vege-
tables for an individual family, and farm animals are the
money crop.

The people in the Promised Land community are less suspicious of strangers than are most rural Southern Negroes.
Since everyone knew "Lawyer Mays," at least by reputation,
we were welcomed as visitors and not treated as intruders. The
farmers soon relaxed and talked freely with us. We interviewed Derquis Moragne Hawes, a 68 year-old mulatto wom-
an, granddaughter of Calvin Moragne, an original settler, and

daughter of Joseph Moragne. She lives on the original home place in the house built by her grandfather, and the descendants of the other six Moragne brothers still live in the immediate vicinity. She and her husband have a garden and raise turkeys and quail, making enough money to meet their needs and those of a grandchild who lives with them. She related bits of family history and gave us the background of the family's land tenure in Promised Land. Seven Moragne brothers (Calvin, Moses, Eli, William, Wade,[15] Andrew, and Isaac) had all acquired land from the Land Commission during Reconstruction. Of the 33 original settlers named in Cardozo's report who were still in residence in 1880, she recognized the names of 19 families: Bradley, Wideman, Fields, Goodwin, Goode, Hurst, Jackson, Litman, Perrin, Reid, Reynolds, Smith, as well as the seven families descended from the Moragne brothers. These nineteen families not only still resided within the tract, but also remained on the original holdings of the families. She told us that of the remaining names on our list, many of their direct descendants continued to live within the community, but the names had changed because it had been the daughters who remained and brought their husbands to live within Promised Land.[16]

Alice Turner Wideman, another resident with whom we talked, was intelligent and well-spoken, and her attitude toward us was not the least strained. Both her family and her husband's family had lived on the Marshall tract since the early years of Reconstruction.[17] Mrs. Wideman's father, John

15. Shortly before taking up residence on the Marshall tract, Eli and Wade Moragne had been seized by a band of Ku Klux Klansmen and beaten with a wagon whip, because they were believed to be "the leading Radicals in the neighborhood" (*Repts. and Resols., 1869–1870*, pp. 1061–1064).

16. Interview with Derquis Moragne Hawes, November 24, 1963.

17. J. H. Turner—her grandfather—settled on the Marshall tract in January, 1870. Her husband's grandfather, Moses Wideman, settled upon the land in October, 1871 (Record of Sales A, Secretary of State's Office).

Turner, had been minister of the Promised Land congregation. When he died in 1933 he left his daughter clear title to the original homestead and deeds for additional acreage he had bought up at the beginning of the depression. The Wideman land appeared more prosperous, their home larger and more comfortable than their neighbors'. Apparently the Widemans were successful farmers. Clear title to the land can be offered as a partial explanation for their prosperity.[18]

Others we interviewed, although not reluctant to talk, had little additional information to offer us. They knew only that their families had resided in Promised Land for many years. Before leaving the settlement we crossed Curtail Creek to visit John Nash, son of Wilson Nash, an original Land Commission settler. Wilson Nash received a Land Commission deed to 85 acres in 1881.[19] John Nash married, left his father's homestead, and moved to a farm just across the boundary of the Marshall tract. When we met, he was 76 years old, knew many of the old settlers, and substantiated much of the information given to us by the two women.[20]

Back in Columbia we attempted to piece together what we had observed in our brief afternoon at Promised Land. In general attitude, these independent Negroes seemed to us less strained and less suspicious of strangers that most of the Negroes we encountered daily. Those we talked to were devoid of the embarrassment often felt by Negroes who have had the color line constantly emphasized in meeting white people. Farming their own land and living in a simple homogeneous community apparently is a powerful factor differentiating them from the majority of their race in their manner toward white people. The possession of land gave them a sense of self-

18. Interview with Alice Turner Wideman, November 24, 1963.
19. Duplicate Titles B, 1881–1887.
20. Interview with John Nash, November 24, 1963.

assurance and a certain feeling of equality, both attitudes usually lacking in black tenants and urban workers in the South.

While tenancy encouraged in Negroes migratory habits to escape the restraints of the color line, the ownership of the soil had anchored Promised Land Negroes to the land for almost a century. These independent farmers have not migrated from farm to farm, from job to job, or from state to state. "They stay put." Moreover, as independent farmers they have had considerably more freedom to diversify and experiment with new crops than tenants are normally allowed.

Furthermore, the settlers, through their continuous support of the church and school within the Negro community, overcame much of their heritage of ignorance. Most of the older residents, we learned from Mr. Mays, had received some elementary education. They are relatively self-assured and appear to be more ambitious than most rural Negroes. Their children, in some instances, have gone on to college and returned to become the leaders within the homogeneous community. Moreover, a former Promised Land resident, the Reverend Benjamin J. Glover, while pastor of the Emmanuel AME Church in Charleston, was one of the Negro leaders in the Charleston demonstrations in the summer of 1963,[21] seeking to gain civil rights for all Negroes throughout the state. (Coincidently, Richard H. Cain the proponent of land reform at the Convention of 1868 had been pastor of the Emmanuel AME Church in Charleston during Reconstruction.)

After 1890, with Negroes excluded from participation

21. Letter from Wylma Wates to the author, November 12, 1964; *The State and the Columbia Record*, May 28, 1967. In 1965, Reverend Glover became president of Allen University in Columbia, S.C.; two years later he was removed from the presidency by the board of trustees for his refusal to dismiss faculty members who participated in a campus boycott. "I couldn't fire them for that. I've done it too much myself," said Glover (*Ibid.*).

in Southern society and with the closed society firmly entrenched, one of the Negroes' overwhelming ambitions was to become relatively self-sufficient by establishing a separate society that would give blacks maximum freedom. In a way, the Land Commission communities[22] may have provided an open end through which Negroes could escape the infantilizing effects of the closed society. It does not seem unreasonable to project that the Land Commission communities might have become self-governing units not unlike colonial New England towns, providing a medium through which Negro leadership could have developed. Indeed, within the boundaries of these black communities they probably were free to develop economically and socially in virtual independence of the whites.

Presumably, the state as well as individuals benefited from these communities. As owners of property blacks have been subject to the same taxes as the whites. The settlers, usually referred to as being a proud and thrifty people, according to Mr. Mays, rarely became welfare cases dependent on state support. In fact, the "black yeomanry" have helped lighten the financial burden of state government. With the rising tide of Negro civil rights, South Carolina may well have need of these self-reliant citizens.

The Promised Land community gave us a glimpse of what might have been, but, in reality, the South Carolina Land Commission experiment must be judged a failure. Overconfident Republican administrators and impatient theorists failed to see that the concept of Negro landownership sponsored by a single state was far ahead of the public thinking of the age. Moreover, the principle of equality in economic matters, though imposed upon South Carolina during Reconstruction, had failed to strike roots in the society. Corruption and venali-

22. No systematic search has been made to find Land Commission communities, but two have been found and others may exist.

ty in the administration of the program further alienated the majority of white South Carolinians, who regarded the Land Commission experiment as a scheme inflicted upon them by Republicans eager to retain the support of the Negro electorate, and they continued to so regard it until its abandonment in the post-Reconstruction era.

But the responsibility for the ultimate betrayal of the concept of Negro landownership rests with the nation. It is impossible to exaggerate how important the possession of land was to the former slaves; nevertheless, Congress failed to come forth with the "promised land." Since confiscation of Southern estates probably would have been an unsatisfactory solution involving constitutional questions and increasing racial bitterness, a meaningful answer might have been found in the introduction by Congress of a large-scale land redistribution program modeled on the Land Commission experiment. Needless to say, the nation made no such commitment, and, as a consequence, the freedman, without land in an agricultural society, found his independence to be ephemeral.

APPENDIX I

Total Number of
Land Commission Settlers

HENRY HAYNE ESTIMATED that 14,000 Negro families had been settled upon the land by 1876.[1] The surveyor of the Land Commission, Benjamin F. Jackson, stated that by February, 1871, between 9,000 and 10,000 persons or approximately 2,000 families were residing on Land Commission tracts.[2] According to Land Commission records, by September, 1872, 5,008 certificates of purchase had been issued.[3] Unfortunately many of Hayne's Land Commission ledger books for 1873–1876, including the records of certificates of purchase, are missing. In 1875 Hayne had reported to the legislature that unless $3,000 were appropriated immediately to rebind the

1. Letter from Henry Hayne to Hon. W. A. Jarray, April 8, 1876, Commission Letters, Secretary of State, 1870–1878, S.C.A.
2. Report of Benjamin F. Jackson to R. C. De Large, February 23, 1871, Land Transfer File, 1866–1877; B. F. Jackson to H. H. Kimpton, February 23, 1871 (misfiled), H. H. Kimpton, Financial Agent, Quarterly Report, 1870, S.C.A.
3. Duplicate Titles A, Secretary of State's Office; Duplicate Certificates B, Secretary of State's Office, S.C.A.; Loose Certificates of Purchase, Drawers 3, 7, 11, 15, 16, 51, Division of General Services, S. C. Record Center, Columbia.

Land Department records they would be beyond repair.[4] In any case, only 1,016 loose certificates of purchase that had been issued after 1872 and before 1877 could be located.[5] Probably more were issued; moreover, since certificates of purchase, except under Cardozo, were assignable only after three years of continuous residence, payment of 6 per cent interest per year, and also all taxes imposed by the state,[6] presumably many more than 6,024 families participated in the experiment, but had not met these requirements and so were not issued certificates. Although I have not found a detailed account disputing Hayne's estimate that in 1876, 14,000 families were in residence, his estimate is open to question. If 14,000 families had divided up equally 112,404.6 acres—the number of acres Secretaries of State Cardozo and Hayne credited to the state as having been purchased by the Land Commission—the average size of a Land Commission lot would have been approximately eight acres. The lots in fact were much larger, varying from a minimum of 7½ acres to a maximum of 100 acres. Hayne's figure is probably based on the number of participants between 1869 and 1876, and not on the number of settlers on the tracts in 1876. Since many occupants forfeited their lands to the state during Hayne's administration, their lands were resold, and new accounts were established for the same lots. Even if Hayne's figure is a generous estimate, based on participants rather than number of families actually in residence in 1876, it is not unreasonable to project that before the experiment was concluded, 14,000 Negro families, or approximately 70,000 persons, had participated in the redistribution program. This latter figure was arrived at through the use of

4. *Repts. and Resols., 1875–1876,* p. 393.
5. Loose Certificates of Purchase, Drawers 17, 23, 66, 68, Division of General Services, S. C. Records Center.
6. *Statutes at Large,* XIV, p. 276.

census records. Locating Land Commission settlers and "counting noses" proved to be tedious and time-consuming. A map of South Carolina issued by the Department of Agriculture of South Carolina in 1883 and indicating the townships and census enumeration districts, was an invaluable aid for locating the Land Commission tracts in their designated enumeration districts of the 1880 census.[7] A representative sampling was set up,[8] and each enumeration district was carefully scanned to locate the settlers. According to the findings, the average Land Commission family consisted of five persons. Thus, the approximate number of Negroes benefiting at one time or another from the land experiment would be 70,000 persons.

7. U. S. Census Records, State of South Carolina, 1880 Population Schedules (Abbeville-York), Microfilm Publications, 27 reels.
8. For method of selection, *see* Appendix II.

APPENDIX II

Land Commission Settlers
in Selected Counties

IN THIS STUDY of the South Carolina Land Commission 14 counties were singled out (1) to ascertain the percentage of settlers holding deeds and certificates of purchase in 1872 still in residence in 1880,[1] (2) to determine whether any tracts were interracial, and (3) to estimate the size of the average Land Commission tract family.[2]

Three criteria were employed in selecting the 19 tracts located in 14 of the 31 counties (Table 1): (1) geographically, the counties containing the largest proportions of Negroes, (2) the ability to locate the tract within a given census enumeration district, and (3) large tracts with a significant number of settlers in residence before 1872. For these purposes, a map of South Carolina (Department of Agriculture of South Carolina, 1883) indicating townships and census enumeration districts provided the means of locating the Land Commission

1. To establish a control, only those names listed in the county agents accounts with settlers before the fall of 1872 are included (Account of Sales A, Secretary of State's Office; Settlement Book, Vol. 3, S.C.A.).
2. *See* Appendix I.

TABLE 1

County	Tract	No. of Holders of Deeds and Certificates of Purchase in 1872*	In Residence in 1880	Race Black	Mulatto	White
Abbeville	Marshall	41	33	27	6	0
Anderson	Fretwell	9	3	2	0	1
Charleston	Cattle Bluff	12	9	9	0	0
Charleston	Greenwich	34	22	22	0	0
Charleston	Rushland	44	29	29	0	0
Charleston	Woodville	36	23	23	0	0
Chester	Brawley	11	6	5	0	1
Chester	Yocum	14	5	3	0	2
Colleton	Heyward	61	30	28	1	1
Fairfield	Harrison River	78	24	18	5	1
Greenville	Cleaveland	32	21	7	0	14
Kershaw	Burroughs	102	48	46	0	2
Lexington	Ensor	24	14	12	0	2
Oconee	Lewis	49	33	20	3	10
Orangeburg	Tynah	42	22	21	1	0
Richland	Hopkins	37	27	20	6	1
Richland	O'Hanlon	71	37	34	1	2
Williamsburg	Cross Roads	31	21	21	0	0
York	Witherspoon	38	17	16	0	1
		776	424	363	23	38

tracts in the 1880 census.[3] Having located the enumeration districts of each tract, I searched the microfilms until the settlers were found. The list of names of Land Commission settlers in each tract under investigation was completed from the Land Commission's records. With so many pitfalls and incalculables in the selection process, it is wise to concede a wide margin for error.

3. U. S. Census Records, State of South Carolina, 1880 Population Schedules (Abbeville-York), Microfilm Publications, 27 reels.

APPENDIX III

Geographic Distribution of Land Commission Tracts

TABLE 2 IS A STATEMENT submitted by Secretary of State Francis L. Cardozo to the South Carolina legislature in November, 1872, giving the number of acres purchased by the Land Commission in each county.

Figure 1 shows South Carolina counties in 1868; the county boundaries were determined by Historical Records Survey, W.P.A., 1938. The map is shaded to show the distribution of Land Commission acres purchased in each county. The key to county numbers is provided in Table 2. Almost half (50,-102.6) of the total number of acres (112,404.6) purchased by the Land Commission were in the five low country counties of Charleston, Colleton, Georgetown, Beaufort, and Williamsburg.

Figure 2 is a plat of the Greenwich tract in Charleston County. In this tract the average lot was 25 acres, whereas in some low country tracts the average lot was 10 acres. The surveyor located the house lots together at one corner of the tract, each house lot being separated from its farming plot. Since this arrangement was unusual, presumably, the Greenwich settlers were occupying the former slave quarters.

Figure 3 is a plat of the Lee tract—one of the five tracts purchased in Spartanburg County from Benjamin F. Bates. The Lee tract contained nine lots averaging 57 acres each, a size similar to most of the Land Commission lots in the region.

Figure 1 **Distribution of Land Commission Land in South Carolina Counties (See Table 1 for key to county numbers.)**

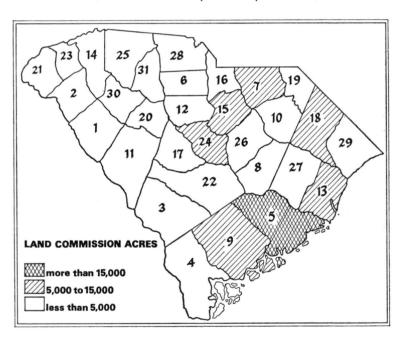

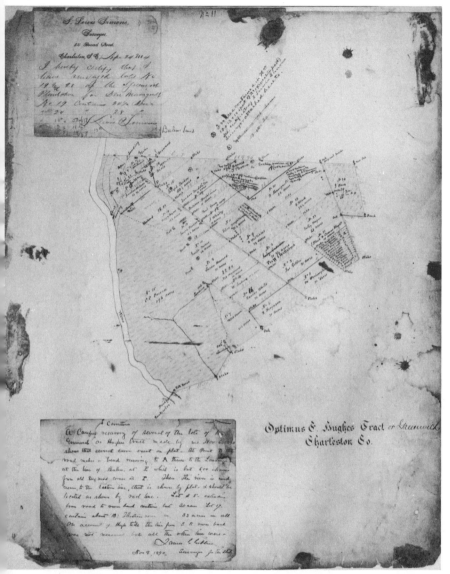

Figure 2 Greenwich Tract, Charleston County

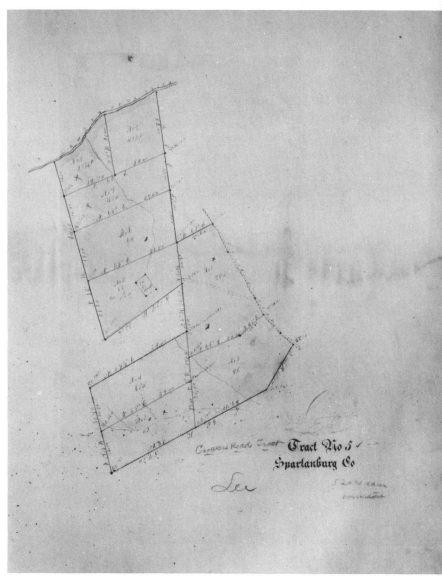

Figure 3 Lee Tract, Spartanburg County

TABLE 2*

Counties	Land Commission Acres
1. Abbeville	2,742
2. Anderson	645
3. Barnwell	842
4. Beaufort	3,275½
5. Charleston	25,501.6
6. Chester	1,251
7. Chesterfield	6,918
8. Clarendon	615
9. Colleton	12,894½
10. Darlington	1,497½
11. Edgefield	2,778
12. Fairfield	4,124
13. Georgetown	6,023
14. Greenville	1,766
15. Kershaw	6,360
16. Lancaster	1,204
17. Lexington	3,273
18. Marion	6,661
19. Marlboro	800
20. Newberry	1,874
21. Oconee	2,010
22. Orangeburg	1,723½
23. Pickens	1,502
24. Richland	9,398
25. Spartanburg	1,972
26. Sumter	454
27. Williamsburg	2,138
28. York	2,362
Totals	112,404.6

* *Repts. and Resols., 1872–1873*, p. 134. No land was reported purchased in Horry (29.), Laurens (30.) and Union (31.) counties.

SELECTED BIBLIOGRAPHY

ALTHOUGH SOUTH CAROLINA's historical agencies have made amazing progress in increasing their collections and housing them adequately since Simkins and Woody published *South Carolina During Reconstruction* in 1932, the holdings of the Reconstruction era remain uneven and scattered. A breakthrough, however, has occurred in the area of public records.

By the Archives Act of 1954 all non-current records were to be turned over to the South Carolina Archives Department. A record management program was begun under the late Director Dr. James Easterby. In its initial stage the program was hampered by the inadequacy of space to house all the documents, but this obstacle was removed with the construction of the State Archives in 1960. In July, 1963, the last boxes of public records were removed from dead storage and transferred to the new building. By mid-1965, approximately 100,-000 papers of the South Carolina governors from James L. Orr through Wade Hampton had been arranged in chronological order.[1] Now researchers have abundant public records at their disposal; their task is simplified further by an enthusiastic archival staff ready to anticipate almost every research need.

1. William L. McDowell, Jr., "Archives News," *The South Carolina Historical Magazine*, 66 (July, 1965), 201.

Briefly, on the subject of the Land Commission, the Archives' holdings include: 36 Land Commission record books; two large plat books; Secretary of State's Letterbook, Land Commission Department, 1872–1878 (the secretary of state assumed the duties of the land commissioner when the latter office was abolished in 1872); 16 Sinking Fund Commission Ledgers (after 1878 the Sinking Fund Commission assumed the responsibility of directing Land Commission sales); Minutes of the Advisory Board to the Land Commission, 1869–1872; and three Minute Books of the Sinking Fund Commission, 1878–1889. The 100,000 papers of the pertinent South Carolina governors—Orr, Scott, Moses, Chamberlain, and Hampton—were examined by this researcher before these papers were arranged by the staff, and much material pertaining to the land experiment was found in them. In the Loose Paper Files, 1866–1877, especially the Land Transfer File and Loose Papers—unfiled, 1866–1877, there is also an abundance of data concerning the operations of the Land Commission.

Of published state records the most useful are *The Proceedings of the Constitutional Convention of 1868*, out of which the Land Commission experiment was conceived, and the *Reports and Resolutions of the General Assembly of South Carolina*, 1869–1890, which contain annual and special reports of the Land Commission. Indispensable were the *Population Schedules* of South Carolina in the census records of 1870 and 1880. By scanning the census county by county, Abbeville through York, I located many Land Commission tracts, ascertained the race of the settlers, and was able to pinpoint the most successful Land Commission communities. The criterion applied for the last named judgment was the number of original settlers still in residence on the tracts in 1880.

Four special works on Reconstruction in South Carolina deserve special acknowledgment for their usefulness to this study: Martin Abbott, *The Freedmen's Bureau in South Carolina, 1865–1872*; Willie Lee Rose, *Rehearsal For Reconstruction: The Port Royal Experiment*; Francis B. Simkins and Robert H. Woody, *South Carolina During Reconstruction*; and Joel Williamson, *After Slavery: The Negro in South Carolina During Reconstruction, 1861–1877*. (Although Williamson's book appeared after the first draft of this manuscript had been completed, it proved to be indispensable for subsequent revisions.)

Many manuscript sources were used and are included in the following selected bibliography.

Primary Sources

LETTERS, MANUSCRIPTS, AND COLLECTED PAPERS

James Butler Campbell Papers. Manuscript Division, South Caroliniana Library, University of South Carolina, Columbia.

Thomas B. Chaplin Manuscript Diary. South Carolina Historical Society, Charleston.

Clifton Plantation Book, 1878–1880. Manuscript Division, South Caroliniana Library, University of South Carolina, Columbia.

Mrs. R. F. Cole to Francis M. Hutson, letter of August 2, 1965. South Carolina Archives, Columbia.

James Conner Papers. South Carolina Historical Society, Charleston.

Francis Warrington Dawson Papers. Manuscript Collections, Duke University, Durham, North Carolina.

Samuel Dibble Papers. Manuscript Collections, Duke University, Durham, North Carolina.

Richard Dozier Papers. Southern Historical Collection, University of North Carolina, Chapel Hill.

Martin Witherspoon Gary Papers, 1851–1927. Manuscript Division, South Caroliniana Library, University of South Carolina, Columbia.

Governors' Papers. Papers of James L. Orr, 1866–1868; Robert K. Scott, 1868–1872; Franklin J. Moses, Jr., 1872–1874; Daniel H. Chamberlain, 1874–1876; Wade Hampton, 1876–1878. South Carolina Archives, Columbia.

Governors' Papers, 1868–1890, unsorted. South Carolina Archives, Columbia.

Wade Hampton's Appointments, County, 1877–1878. South Carolina Archives, Columbia.

Wade Hampton Letterbook, Miscellaneous, 1878–1879. South Carolina Archives, Columbia.

Wade Hampton Papers. Manuscript Division, South Caroliniana Library, University of South Carolina, Columbia.

Reuben G. Holmes Papers. Manuscript Division, South Caroliniana Library, University of South Carolina, Columbia.

"Charles Howard Family Domestic History," privately typed, reproduced, and bound. Copies are in the South Carolina Archives and the Southern Historical Collection.

Loose Papers File, 1868–1877. South Carolina Archives, Columbia. In the Loose Papers File are personal letters to state officials as well as affidavits, appointments, impeachments, land transfers, petitions, reports, and resolutions.

Loose Papers, 1868–1877, unsorted. South Carolina Archives, Columbia.

Mackay Family Papers, 1822–1926. Manuscript Division, South Caroliniana Library, University of South Carolina, Columbia.

Joseph Warren Waldo Marshall Collection. Manuscript Collections, Duke University, Durham, North Carolina.

Robert McKay Scrapbook, 1865–1887, "South Carolina Redeemed." Manuscript Division, South Caroliniana Library, University of South Carolina, Columbia.

Orr-Patterson Papers. Southern Historical Collection, University of North Carolina, Chapel Hill.

Pinckney Island 1868 Petition. Southern Historical Collection, University of North Carolina, Chapel Hill.

Y. J. Pope to Wade Hampton, Letter of December 23, 1876, unfiled. South Carolina Archives, Columbia.

Henry W. Ravenel Private Journal, 1859–1883. Manuscript Division, South Caroliniana Library, University of South Carolina, Columbia.

Reconstruction Scrapbook, 1865–1877. Manuscript Division, South Caroliniana Library, University of South Carolina, Columbia.

Henry Shelton Sanford Papers. General Sanford Memorial Library, Sanford, Florida. Microfilm.

Jacob F. Schirmer Diary, 1861–1880. South Carolina Historical Society, Charleston.

Yates Snowden Collection. Manuscript Division, South Caroliniana Library, University of South Carolina, Columbia.

Spartanburg County Wills, Book D, 1840–1858. Columbia: W.P.A., 1934, typewritten copy, South Carolina Archives, Columbia.

Edward M. Stoeber Papers, 1864–1869. Manuscript Division, South Caroliniana Library, University of South Carolina, Columbia.

George B. Tindall to Dr. J. Harold Easterby, letter of November 3, 1951, unfiled. South Carolina Archives, Columbia.

Wylma Wates to the author, letter of November 12, 1964.

UNPUBLISHED LAND COMMISSION RECORDS IN THE
SOUTH CAROLINA ARCHIVES, COLUMBIA

Ledgers

Purchase Book, Land Commissioner's Office.
Record of Sales of Land to the Land Commission.
Record of Sales, Office Secretary of State, S.C.L.C.
Account of Sales A, Secretary of State's Office.
Duplicate Certificates A, Land Commissioner, S.C.
Duplicate Certificates C, Land Commissioner, S.C.
Duplicate Titles A, Secretary of State.
Office Secretary of State, Duplicate Titles A.
Duplicate Certificates B, Secretary of State's Office.
Duplicate Titles B, 1881–1887.
Duplicate Titles C, State of South Carolina, 1887–1924.
Tax Titles A, 1881–1885.
Tax Titles B, 1882–1886.
Direct Index Tax Titles C, 1885–1896.
Tax Titles D, 1886–1887, 1891.
Tax Titles E.
Settlement Book, Vol. 3.

Abstract of Forfeited Lands, 1881–1893.
Record, Sinking Fund Book B.
Forfeited Land Reports.
Returns of Land Commission Agents.

Minute Books

Advisory Board Minutes, October 6, 1869–April 1, 1872.
Minutes of the Board of Commissioners' Sinking Fund Commission, 1879–1883.
Secretary of State's Copy of Sinking Fund Minutes, Book "B," December 8, 1882–June 3, 1884.
Minutes of the Sinking Fund Commission, 1883–April 9, 1889.

Miscellaneous

Commission Letters, 1870–1878, Secretary of State, Land Department.
Day Book A, Secretary of State, Land Commission Office, March 25, 1872–October 31, 1873.
Land Commission Letterbook 1, January 4, 1879–August 2, 1881.
Public Land Plats, Book 1, 1857, 1869–1899, 1909, 1918.
Sinking Fund Commission Letterbook 2, March 1, 1881–August 12, 1882.

UNPUBLISHED LAND COMMISSION RECORDS IN THE DIVISION OF GENERAL
SERVICES, SOUTH CAROLINA RECORDS CENTER, COLUMBIA

Loose Certificates of Purchase, 1872–1877.
Loose Letters on Land Commission, 1869–1880.

PUBLISHED RECORDS AND DOCUMENTS

Publications of the United States Government.

Congressional Globe, 1871.
Ku Klux Conspiracy:The Testimony Taken by the Joint Select Committee to Inquire into the Condition of Affairs in the Late Insurrectionary States. Vols. III, IV, and V. Washington: Government Printing Office, 1872.
U. S. Census Records. *State of South Carolina, 1870 Population Schedules (Abbeville-York).* 27 reels, Microfilm Publications.
U. S. Census Records. *State of South Carolina, 1880 Population Schedules (Abbeville-York).* 27 reels, Microfilm Publications.

U. S. House of Representatives. *A Centennial Fourth of July Democratic Celebration. The Massacre of Six Colored Citizens of United States at Hamburg, South Carolina, July 4, 1876.* Debate on Hamburg Massacre, July 15 and 18, 1876.

U. S. House of Representatives. Miscellaneous Documents. *Recent Election in South Carolina: Testimony Taken by the Select Committee on the Recent Election in South Carolina.* No. 31, 44th Cong., 2nd Sess. Washington: Government Printing Office, 1877.

U. S. Senate. Miscellaneous Documents. *South Carolina in 1876: Testimony As to the Denial of the Elective Franchise in South Carolina at the Election of 1875 and 1876.* No. 48, 44th Cong., 2nd Sess. 3 vols. Washington: Government Printing Office, 1877.

U. S. War Department. *Official Records of the War of the Rebellion.* 130 vols. Washington: Government Printing Office, 1880–1891.

Publications of the South Carolina Government and Subordinate Units

Acts and Joint Resolutions of the General Assembly of the State of South Carolina. 1866–1890.

Biographical Directory of the Senate of the State of South Carolina, 1776–1964. Columbia: South Carolina Archives Department, 1964.

Code of Laws of South Carolina, 1952.

Department of Agriculture. *Map of South Carolina,* 1883.

General Statutes and the Code of Civil Procedure for the State of South Carolina, 1881–1882.

Journal of the House of Representatives of the General Assembly of the State of South Carolina, 1868–1890.

Journal of the Senate of the General Assembly of the State of South Carolina, 1868–1890.

Proceedings of the Constitutional Convention of South Carolina, 1868. Charleston: John W. Denny & Co., 1868.

Proceedings of the Taxpayers' Convention of South Carolina, 1871. Charleston: Edward Perry, Printer, Booksellers, and Stationer, 1871.

Reports and Resolutions of the General Assembly of the State of South Carolina, 1868–1890.

Reports of Cases Heard and Determined by the Supreme Court of South Carolina, 1876–1880.

State Board of Agriculture of South Carolina. *South Carolina Resources and Population, Institutions and Industries.* Charleston: Walker, Evans and Cogswell, 1883.

State Council of Defense. *The Growth and Distribution of Population in South Carolina.* Bulletin No. 11. Columbia: Industrial Development Committee, 1943.

Statutes at Large of South Carolina, 1866–1890.

NEWSPAPERS AND PERIODICALS

Anderson *Intelligencer.*
Camden *Journal.*
Charleston *Daily Courier.*
Charleston *Daily News.*
Charleston *Daily Republican.*
Charleston *News and Courier.*
Charleston *Tri-Weekly Courier.*
Columbia *Daily Phoenix.*
Fairfield *Herald* (Winnsboro, S.C.).
Greenville *Enterprise.*
Greenville *Enterprise and Mountaineer.*
Laurensville *Herald.*
The Nation (New York).
Newberry *Herald.*
New York Times.
New York *Tribune.*
Orangeburg *News and Times.*
Spartanburg *Herald.*
The State And The Columbia Record, May 28, 1967.
Winnsboro *News.*

AUTHOR'S PERSONAL INTERVIEWS

Greenwood, South Carolina. Personal interview with Mr. Calhoun Mays, Sr., Chairman of the South Carolina Archives Commission. November 24, 1963.

Greenwood, South Carolina. Personal interview with Mrs. Marshall Mays. November 24, 1963.

Hilton Head, South Carolina. Personal interview with Mrs. Marshall Mays and Mr. Calhoun Mays, Sr., October 9, 1963.
Promised Land, South Carolina. Personal interview with Derquis Moragne Hawes. November 24, 1963.
Promised Land, South Carolina. Personal interview with John Nash. November 24, 1963.
Promised Land, South Carolina. Personal interview with Alice Turner Wideman. November 24, 1963.

Secondary Sources

GENERAL WORKS AND SPECIAL STUDIES

Abbott, Martin L. "The Freedmen's Bureau in South Carolina, 1865–1872." Unpublished Ph.D. dissertation, Department of History, Emory University, 1954. Published by the University of North Carolina Press, 1967.
Allen, Walter. *Governor Chamberlain's Administration in South Carolina.* New York: G. P. Putnam, 1888.
Avary, Myrta Lockett. *Dixie After the War.* New York: Doubleday, Page & Co., 1906.
Ball, William Watts. *The State that Forgot: South Carolina's Surrender to Democracy.* Indianapolis: Bobbs-Merrill Co., 1932.
Bentley, George R. *A History of the Freedmen's Bureau.* Philadelphia: University of Pennsylvania Press, 1955.
Carter, Hodding. *The Angry Scar: The Story of Reconstruction.* New York: Doubleday and Co., 1959.
Cooper, William J., Jr. *The Conservative Regime: South Carolina, 1877–1890.* Baltimore: John Hopkins Press, 1968.
Coulter, E. Merton. *The South During Reconstruction, 1865–1877.* Baton Rouge: Louisiana State University Press, 1947.
Cox, Samuel S. *Union-Disunion-Reunion: Three Decades of Federal Legislation, 1855–1885.* Providence: J. A. and R. A. Reid Publishers, 1888.
Croushore, James H., and Potter, David M. (eds.). *John William*

DeForest, A Union Officer in the Reconstruction. New Haven: Yale University Press, 1948.

Du Bois, W. E. Burghardt. *Black Reconstruction, 1860–1880.* Philadelphia: Albert Saifer, 1935.

Durden, Robert Franklin. *James Shepherd Pike: Republicanism and the American Negro, 1850–1882.* Durham: Duke University Press, 1957.

Emilio, Luis F. *History of the Fifty-Fourth Regiment of Massachusetts Volunteer Infantry, 1863–1865.* Boston: The Boston Book Company, 1894.

Fleming, Walter Lynwood. *The Sequel of Appomattox.* New Haven: Yale University Press, 1919.

Henry, Robert Selph. *The Story of Reconstruction.* Indianapolis: Bobbs-Merrill Co., 1938.

Heyward, Duncan Clinch. *Seed from Madagascar.* Chapel Hill: The University of North Carolina Press, 1937.

Holland, Rupert Sargent (ed.). *Letters and Diary of Laura M. Towne: Written from the Sea Islands of South Carolina, 1862–1884.* Cambridge: The Riverside Press, 1912.

Horn, Stanley F. *Invisible Empire: The Story of the Ku Klux Klan, 1866–1871.* Boston: Houghton Mifflin Co., 1939.

Jarrell, Hampton M. *Wade Hampton and the Negro: The Road Not Taken.* Columbia: University of South Carolina Press, 1949.

Johnson, Guion Griffis. *A Social History of the Sea Islands: With Special Reference to St. Helena Island, South Carolina.* Chapel Hill: The University of North Carolina Press, 1930.

Kibler, Lillian A. *Benjamin F. Perry: South Carolina Unionist.* Durham: Duke University Press, 1946.

Landrum, J. B. O. *History of Spartanburg County.* Atlanta: The Franklin Printing Co., 1900.

McKitrick, Eric L. *Andrew Johnson and Reconstruction.* Chicago: The University of Chicago Press, 1960.

Pearson, Elizabeth Ware (ed.). *Letters from Port Royal Written at the Time of the Civil War.* Boston: W. B. Clarke Co., 1906.

Pease, William H., and Pease, Jane H. *Black Utopia: Negro Communal Experiments in America.* Madison: The State Historical Society of Wisconsin, 1963.

Reynolds, John Schreiner. *Reconstruction in South Carolina, 1865–1877.* Columbia: The State, 1905.

Robertson, Ben. *Red Hills and Cotton: An Upcountry Memory.* New York: Alfred A. Knopf, 1942.

Rose, Willie Lee. *Rehearsal for Reconstruction: The Port Royal Experiment.* New York: Bobbs-Merrill Company, 1964.

Sass, Herbert Ravenel. *Outspoken: 150 Years of the News and Courier.* Columbia: University of South Carolina Press, 1953.

Sheppard, William Arthur. *Red Shirts Remembered.* Atlanta: Ruralist Press, Inc., 1940.

———. *Some Reasons Why Red Shirts Remembered.* Greer, South Carolina: 1940.

Simkins, Francis Butler. *Pitchfork Ben Tillman: South Carolinian.* Baton Rouge: Louisiana State University Press, 1944.

Simkins, Francis Butler, and Woody, Robert Hillary. *South Carolina During Reconstruction.* Chapel Hill: The University of North Carolina Press, 1932.

Simmons, William J. *Men of Mark: Eminent Progressive and Rising.* Cleveland: George M. Rewell and Co., 1887.

Singletary, Otis A. *Negro Militia and Reconstruction.* Austin: University of Texas Press, 1957.

Smith, Daniel Elliott Huger. *A Charlestonian's Recollections, 1846–1913.* Charleston: Carolina Art Association, 1950.

Snowden, Yates (ed.). *History of South Carolina.* New York: The Lewis Publishing Co., 1920.

Stampp, Kenneth M. *The Era of Reconstruction, 1865–1877.* New York: Alfred A. Knopf, 1965.

Taylor, Alruthus Ambush. *The Negro in South Carolina During Reconstruction.* Washington: Association for the Study of Negro Life and History, 1924.

Thompson, Henry Tazewell. *Ousting the Carpetbagger from South Carolina.* Columbia: R. L. Bryan, 1926.

Tindall, George Brown. *South Carolina Negroes, 1877–1900.* Columbia: University of South Carolina Press, 1952.

Trowbridge, J. T. *The South: A Journey Through the Desolated States and Talks with the People.* Hartford: L. Stebbins, 1866.

Wallace, David Duncan. *The History of South Carolina.* 4 vols. New York: American Historical Society, 1934.

Wells, Edward L. *Hampton and Reconstruction.* Columbia: The State Company, 1907.

White, Leonard D. *The Republican Era, 1869–1901*. New York: The Macmillan Co., 1958.

Williams, Alfred Brockenbrough. *Hampton and His Red Shirts: South Carolina's Deliverance in 1876*. Charleston: Walker, Evans & Cogswell Company, 1935.

Williamson, Joel. *After Slavery: The Negro in South Carolina During Reconstruction, 1861–1877*. Chapel Hill: The University of North Carolina Press, 1965.

Woodward, C. Vann. *Origins of the New South, 1877–1913*. Baton Rouge: Louisiana State University Press, 1951.

———. *The Strange Career of Jim Crow*. New York: Oxford University Press, 1955.

Woofter, Thomas J. *Black Yeomanry: Life on St. Helena Island*. New York: Henry Holt and Co., 1930.

ARTICLES

Abbott, Martin. "County Officers in South Carolina in 1868," *The South Carolina Historical Magazine*, LX (January, 1959), pp. 30–40.

———. "Free Land, Free Labor, and the Freedmen's Bureau," *Agricultural History*, XXX (1956), pp. 150–56.

———. "The Freedmen's Bureau and Its Carolina Critics," *Proceedings of the South Carolina Historical Association*, (1962), pp. 15–23.

Chamberlain, Daniel H. "Reconstruction and the Negro," *North American Review*, CXXVII (February, 1879), pp. 161–73.

Grantham, Dewey W., Jr. "The Southern Bourbons Revisited," *South Atlantic Quarterly*, LX (Summer, 1961), pp. 286–95.

McDowell, William L., Jr. "Archives News," *The South Carolina Historical Magazine*, XLVI (July, 1965), pp. 200–02.

Post, Louis F. "A Carpetbagger in South Carolina," *Journal of Negro History*, X (January, 1925), pp. 10–79.

Scroggs, Jack B. "Southern Reconstruction, A Radical View," *Journal of Southern History*, XXIV (November, 1958), pp. 407–29.

Simkins, Francis B. "New Viewpoints of Southern Reconstruction," *Journal of Southern History*, V (February, 1939), pp. 49–61.

Sweat, Edward F. "Francis L. Cardozo: Profile of Integrity in Reconstruction Politics," *Journal of Negro History*, XLVI (January, 1961), pp. 217–32.

Trelease, Allen W. "Who Were the Scalawags?" *Journal of Southern History*, XXIX (November, 1963), pp. 445–68.

Weisberger, Bernard A. "The Dark and Bloody Ground of Reconstruction Historiography," *Journal of Southern History*, XXV (November, 1959), pp. 427–47.

Woody, Robert H. "Franklin J. Moses, Jr., Scalawag Governor of South Carolina, 1872–74," *The North Carolina Historical Review*, X (April, 1933), pp. 111–32.

———. "The South Carolina Election of 1870," *The North Carolina Historical Review*, VIII (1931), pp. 168–86.

INDEX

46, 63, 64; as secretary of state, 84, 89–94, 126, 127, 158; reports by, 92–94, 96, 149, 152, 165, 167; indictment of, 123n
Cardozo, Francis Lewis, Jr., 89n
Cardozo, Henry, 42n
Carolina National Bank, 62
Carolina Spartan, 128
Carpenter, L. Cass, 123n
Carpenter, Richard B., 67, 70–71, 72
Cattle Bluff Tract, 83n, 162
Chamberlain, Daniel H., proponent of Negro landownership, 20–21; as Advisory Board member, 30–31, 35, 58–60, 72; background of, 33–34; as governor, 34, 54, 101–2, 106, 107, 108, 111, 112, 113–14; and frauds, 62, 63–64, 104–5, 131–32
Charleston, S.C., xiii, 9, 29–30, 32, 34, 60, 68, 71, 75, 81, 101, 109, 154
Charleston County, Negro land cooperatives in, 17–19; Land Commission lands in: purchase of, 42n, 48, 57, 59–65, 83n, sale of, 127n, 140, 144, description of, 162, 165, 167; Negro support for Hampton in, 115
Charleston Land Company, 18
Charleston *News*, 56
Charleston *News and Courier*, 101, 104, 106, 109
Chase, Salmon P., 2, 3, 6
Cheraw, S.C., 71
Chester County, 42n, 98, 162, 167
Chesterfield County, 40, 42n, 71, 127, 134, 167
Clarendon County, 97, 167
Cleaveland Tract, 98, 162
Cochran, John R., sale of lands by, 48, 54–56, 75; and frauds, 48, 54–56, 57, 121–22
Colleton County, Negro cooperatives in, 17–18; Land Commission lands in: purchase of, 48, 57, 60–63, 83n, 129, sales of, 127n, 140, 143, description of, 162, 165, 167
Columbia, S.C., 41, 69, 70, 85, 100, 118, 122

Commissioners of Public Lands, 22–24
Committee on Public Lands, 73
Conner, James, 123n, 136n
Conservatives, political action of, xii, 26–27, 66–67, 88, 100, 101, 102, 106, 110, 111; reaction of, to Land Commission, 29–30, 34, 35–36, 47, 148
Constitution of 1868, 22, 25–26
Cook, Mrs. S. S., 36n
Cooperative land experiments, 17–19
Coosaw Island Tract, 115
Corbin, D. T., 87–88
Croft Tract, 39–40
Cross Roads Tract, 133, 162

D

Darlington County, 42n, 167
Davis, Colonel H. C., 39
Dawson, Francis P., 109
Delany, Martin R., 100–1
De Large, Robert C., frauds of, 51–53, 75, 79, 121, 127; and appointment of Negro land commissioner, 58–59; as land commissioner, 62, 65, 72, 74, 75–76, 77–78; background of, 75; subsequent career of, 76, 88
Democratic Party, and Land Commission, 39–40, 103, 122, 130–31, 132–34; in campaign of 1876, 111–17; differences in, 119–20, 124–26. *See also* Conservatives, Redeemers
Dennis, John B., 79n
DeSaussure, Louis, 61
Dibble, Samuel, 121–22
Direct Tax Commission, 9, 11, 12
Donaldson, Robert J., 40, 42n, 71
Du Bois, W.E.B., xv
Dukes, Peter, 142

E

Easterby, J. Harold, 125
Edgefield, S.C., 64, 111
Edgefield County, 35–36, 42n, 67, 142, 167
Edisto Island, 9, 19, 38
Edmonds, Dr. R. H., 27n
Eight Box Law, 137